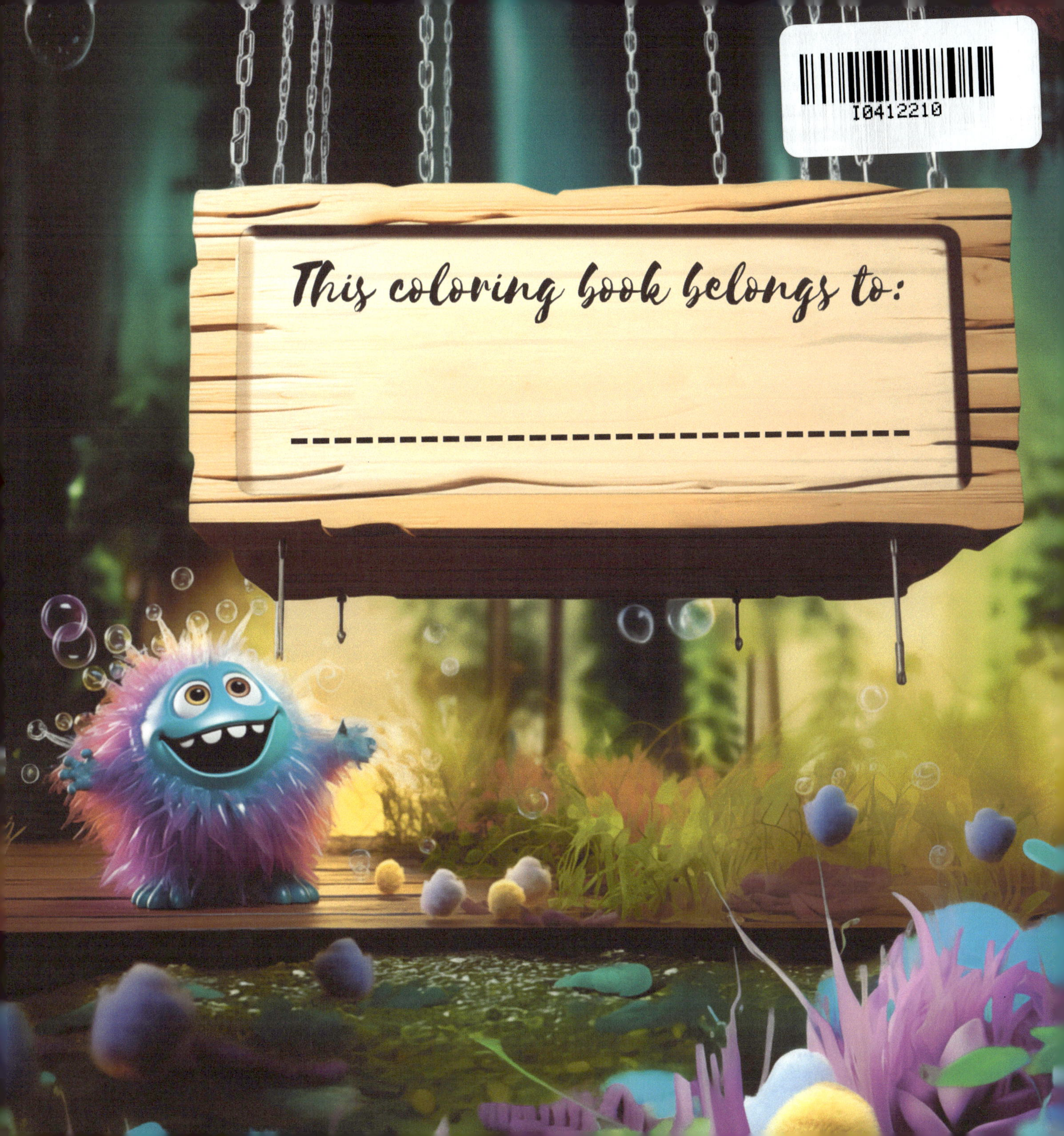
This coloring book belongs to:

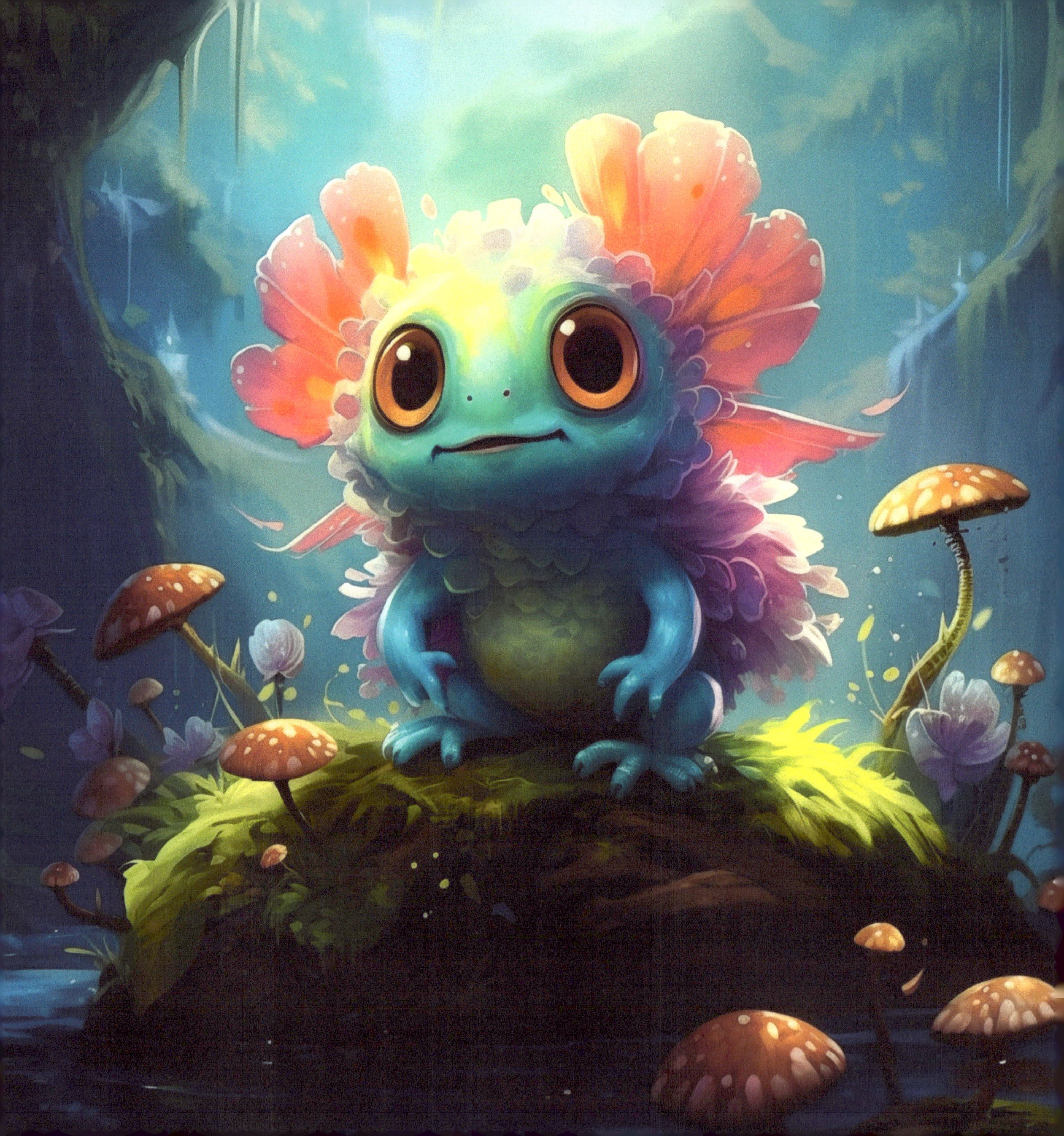

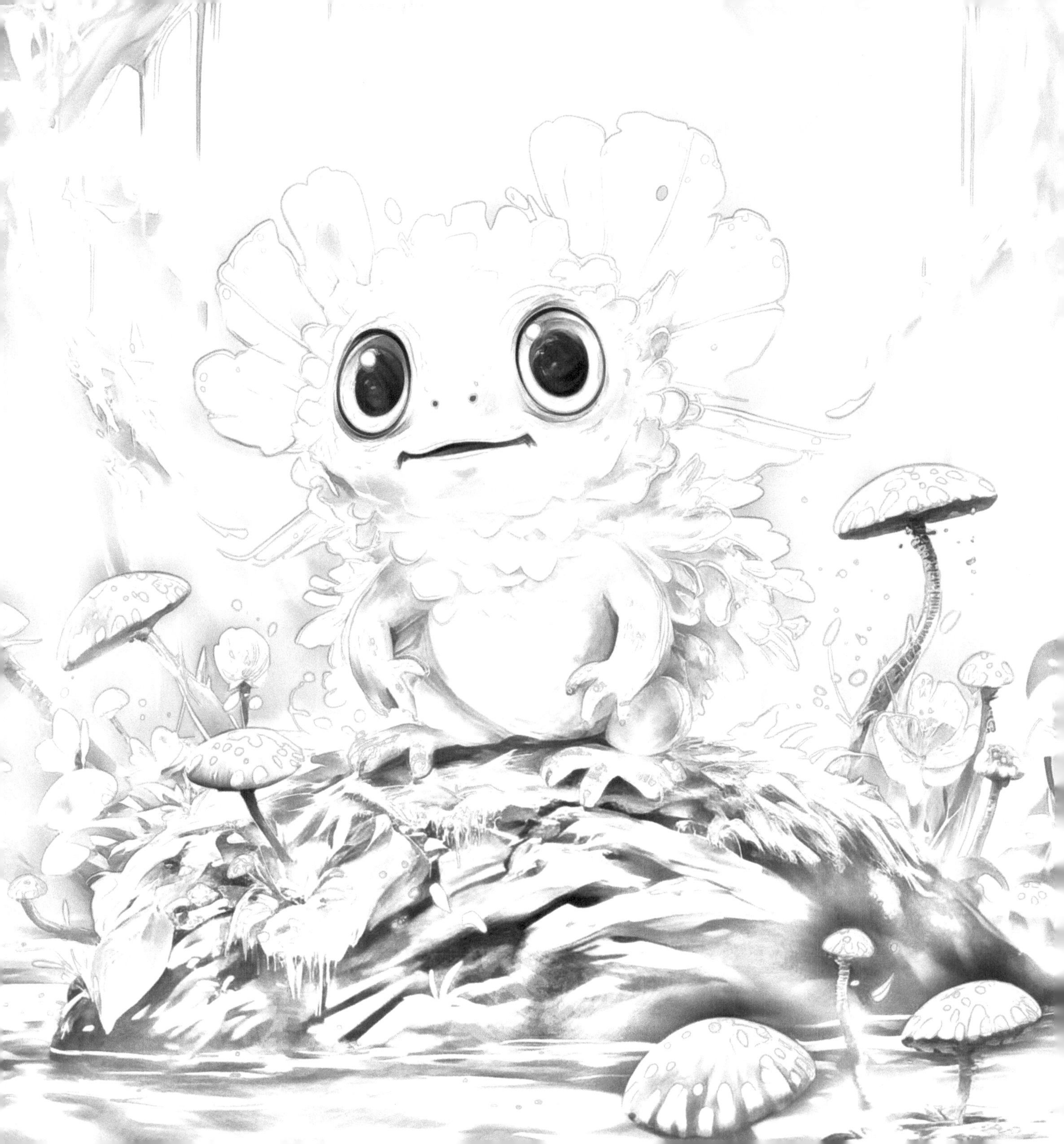

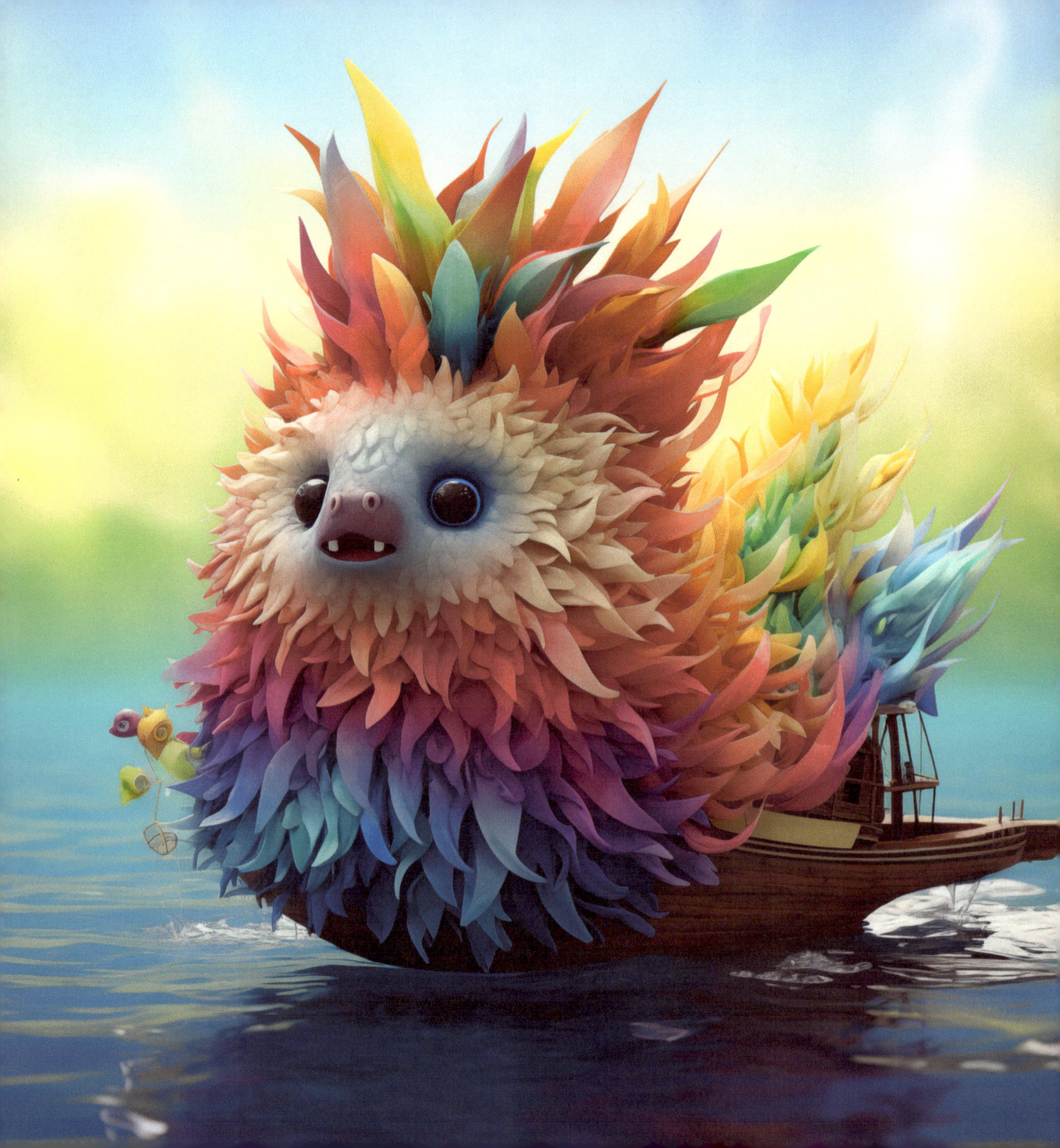

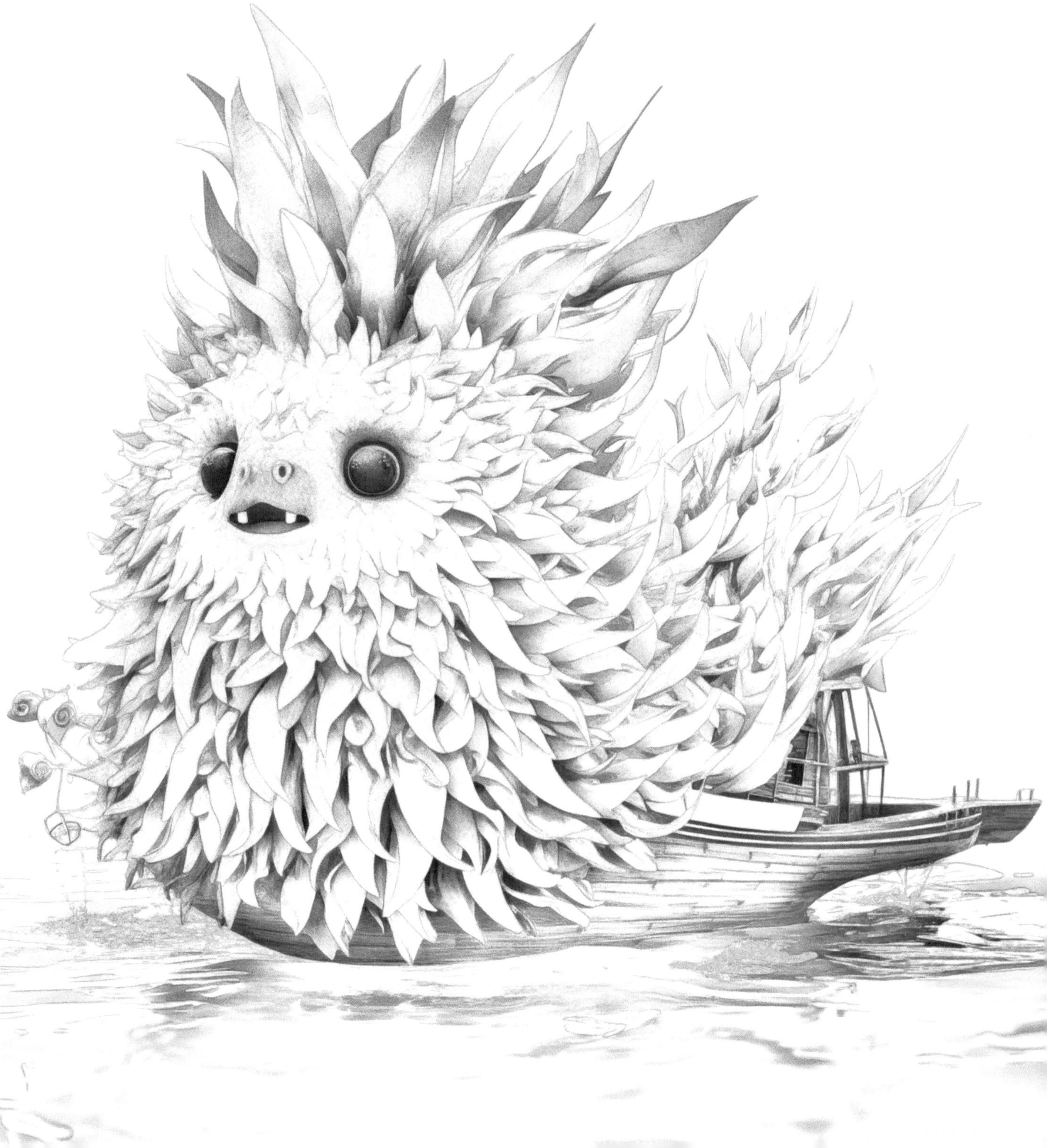

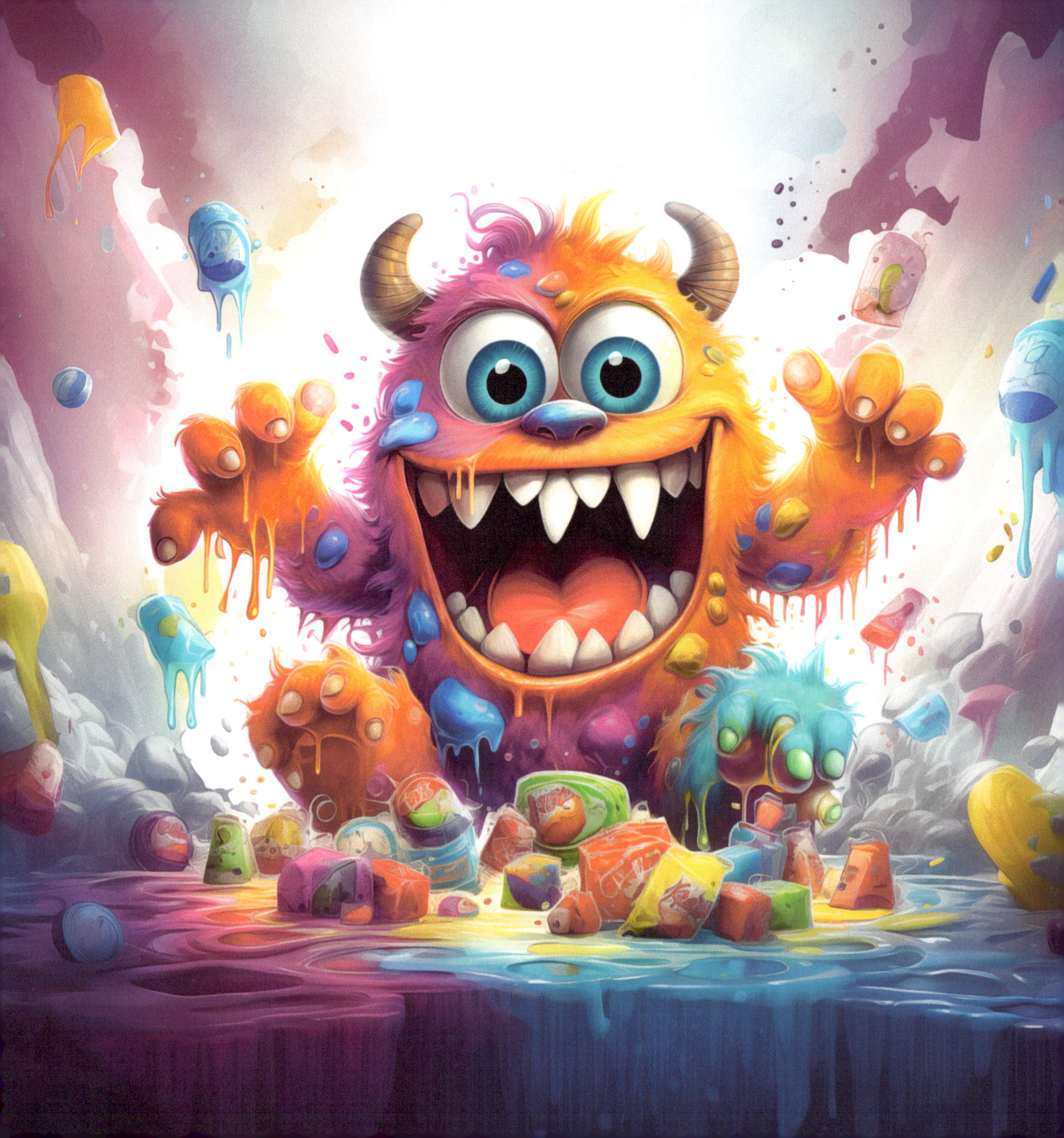

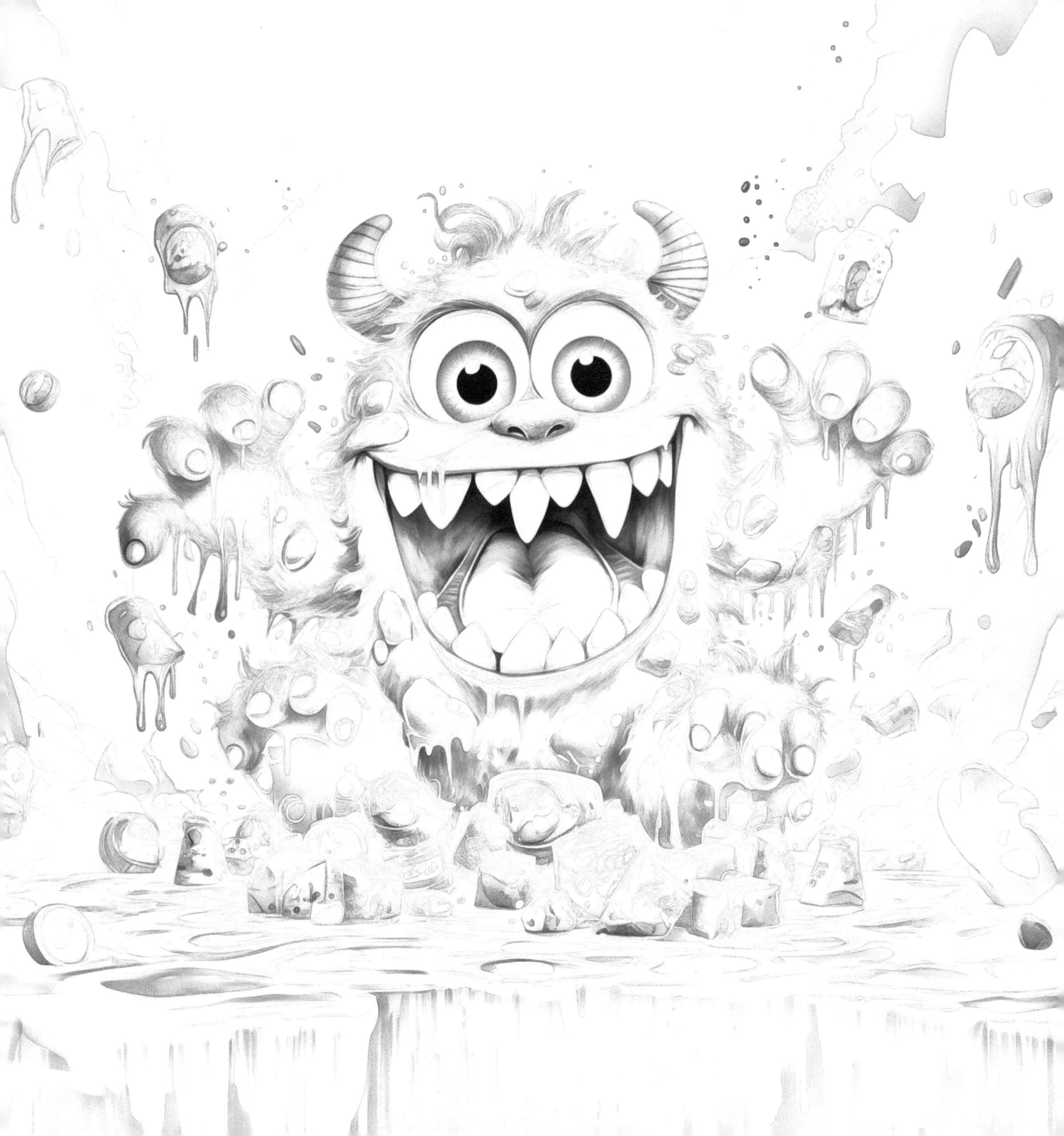

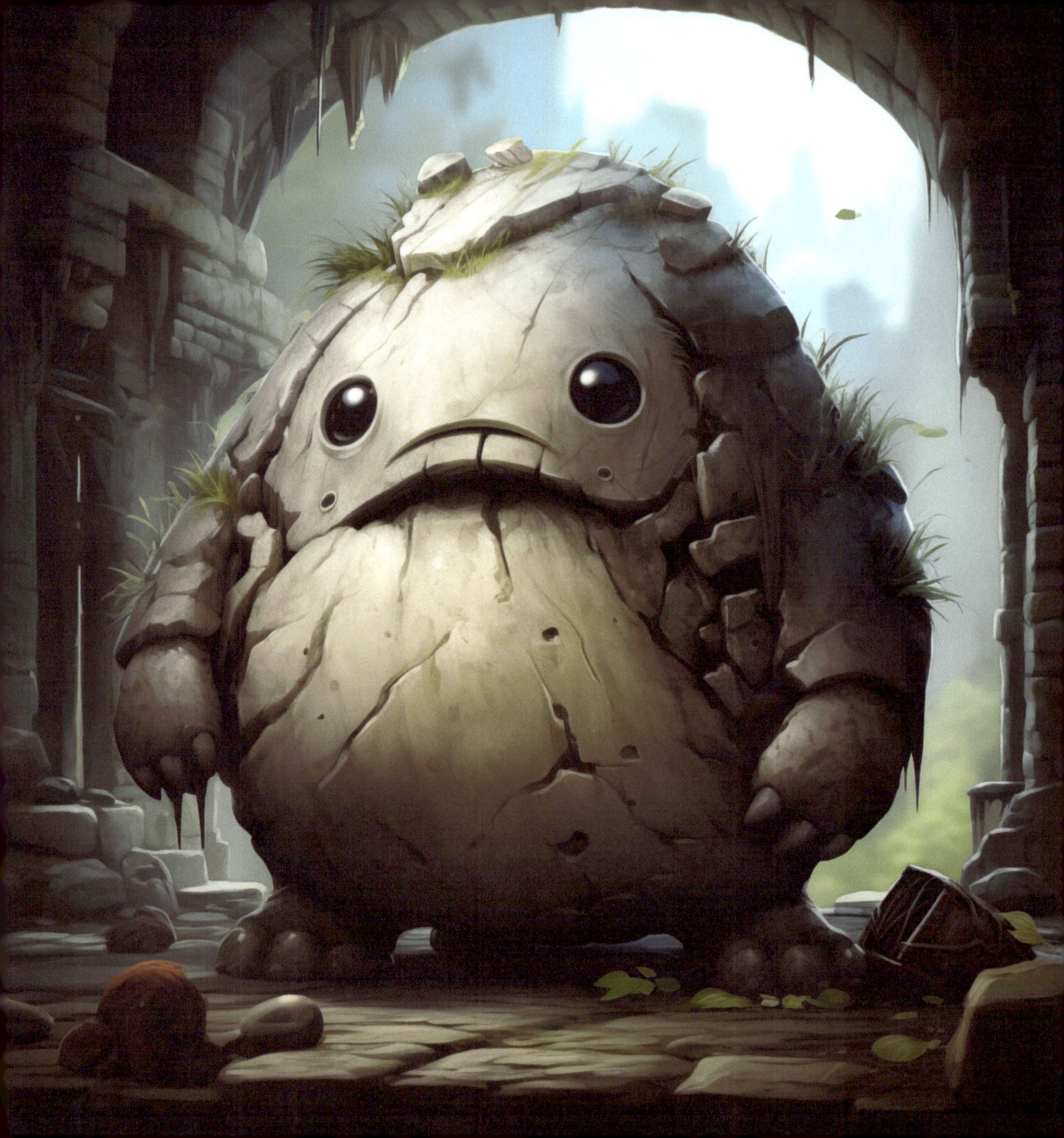

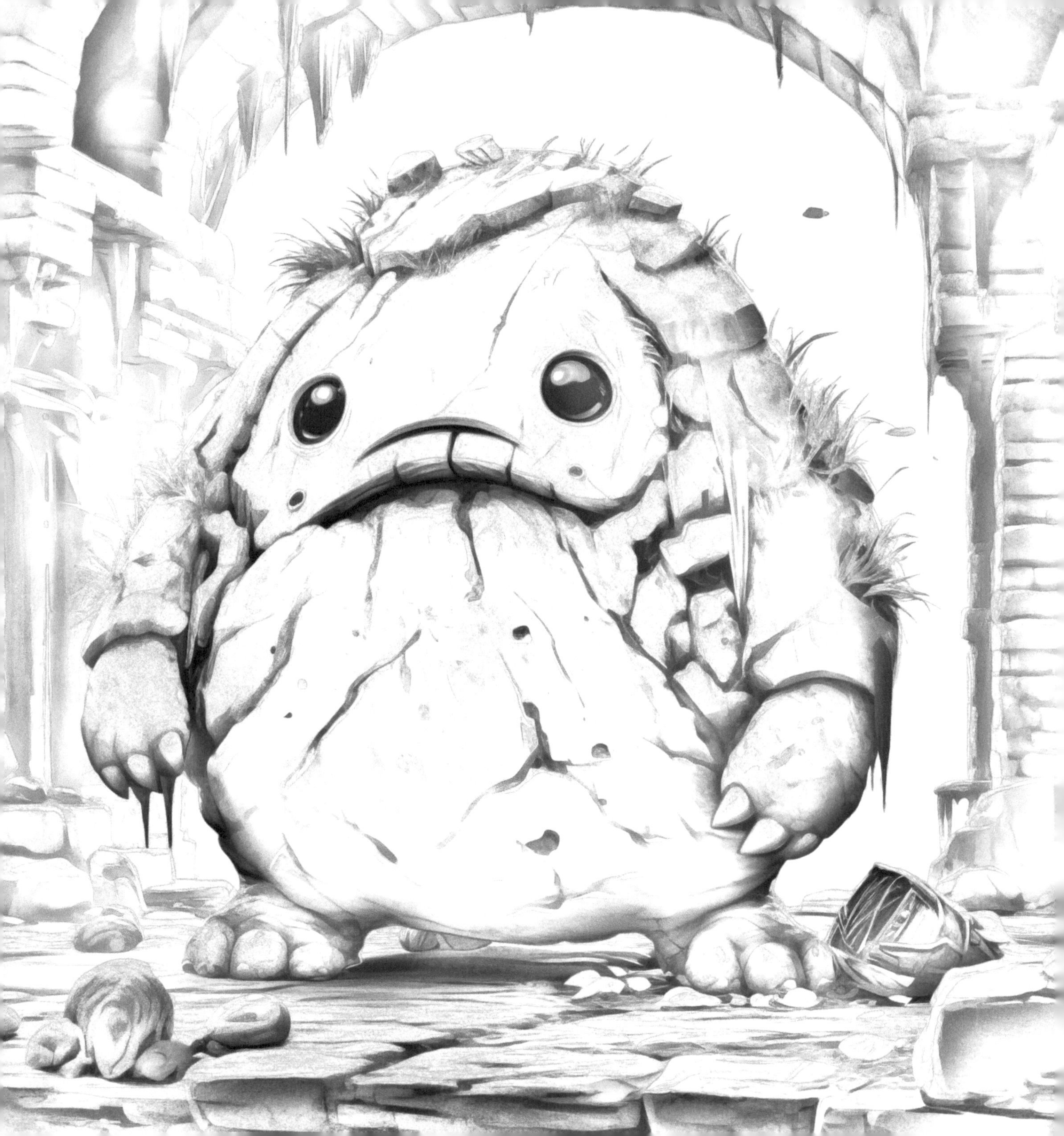

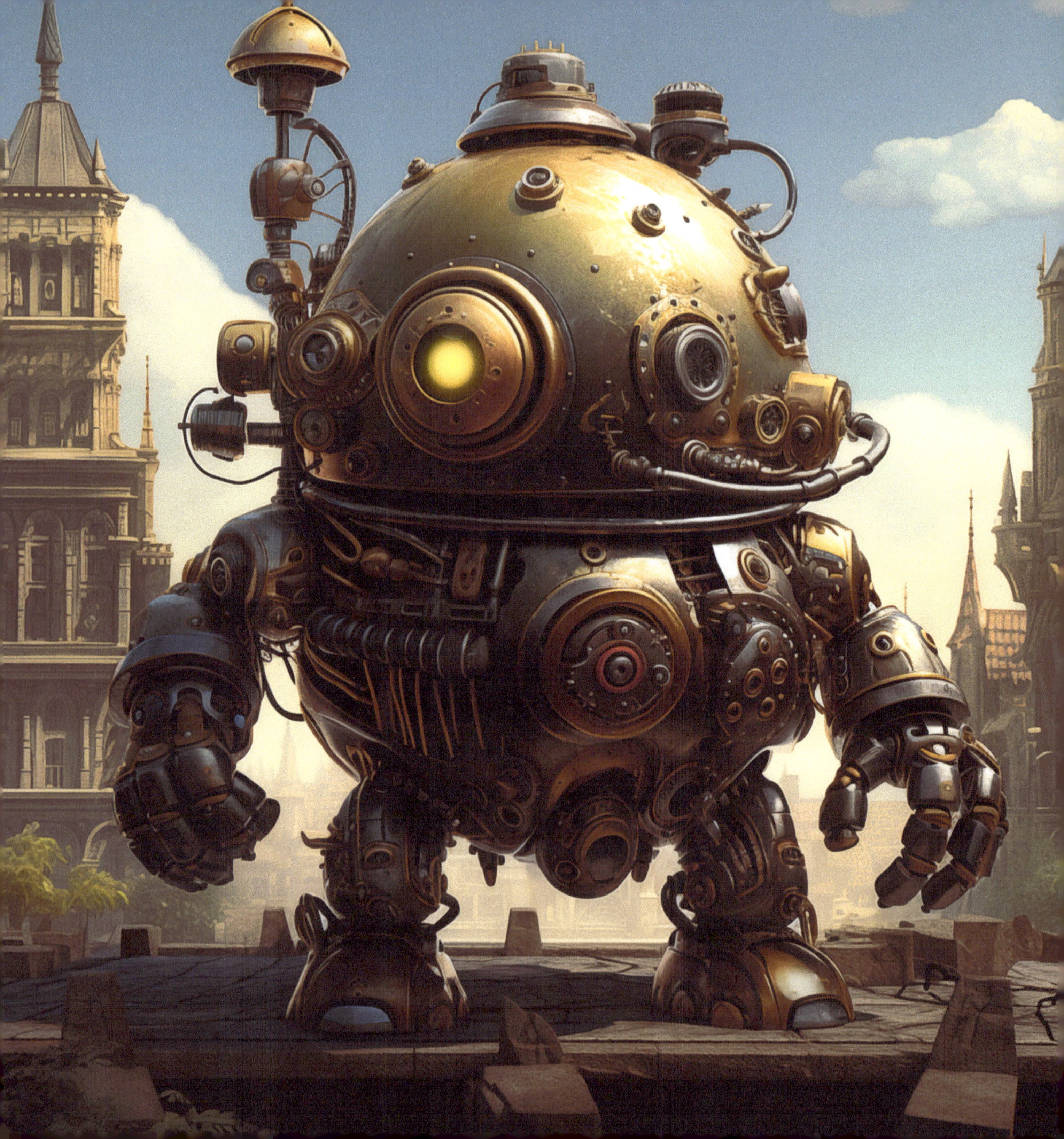

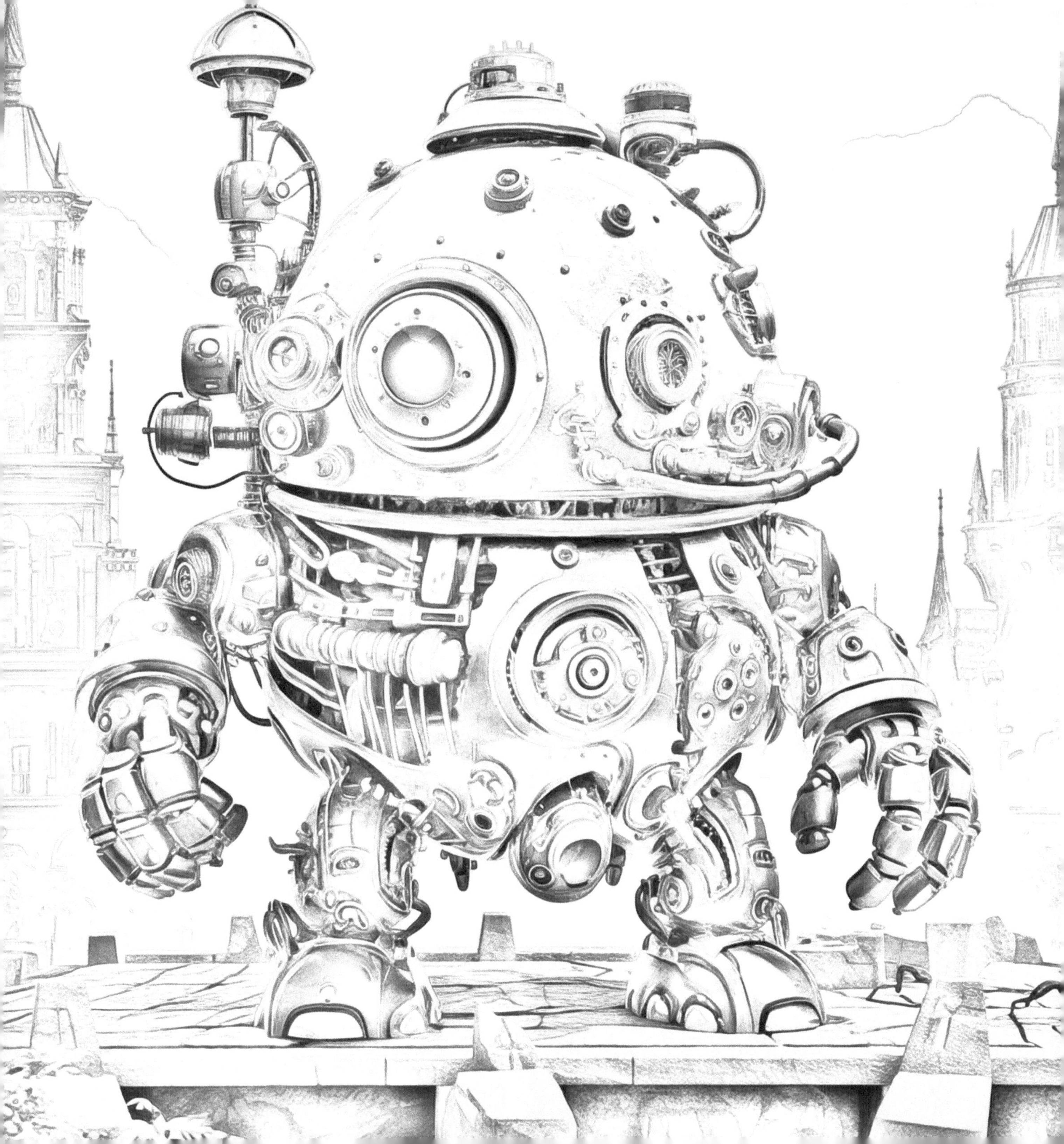

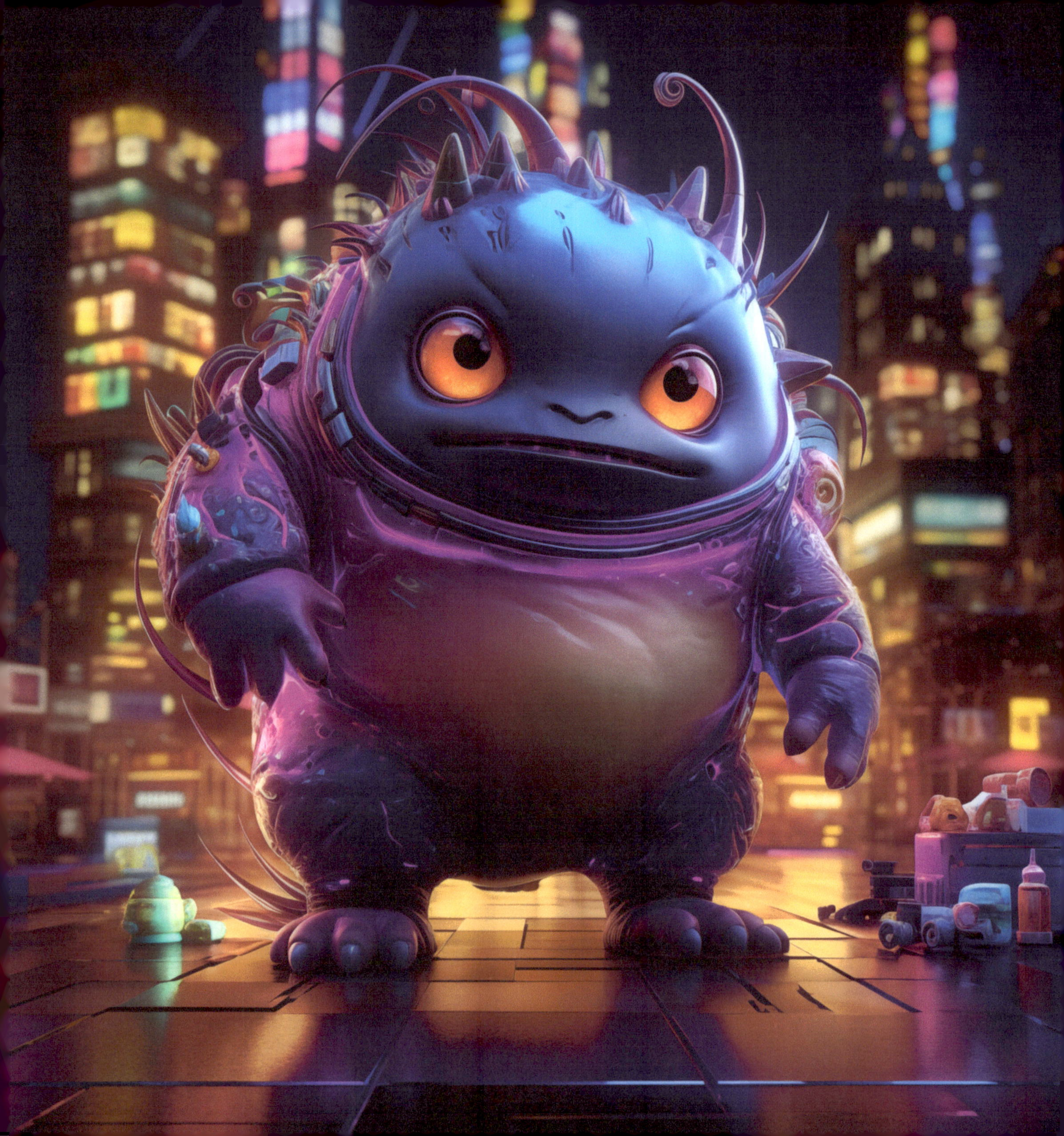

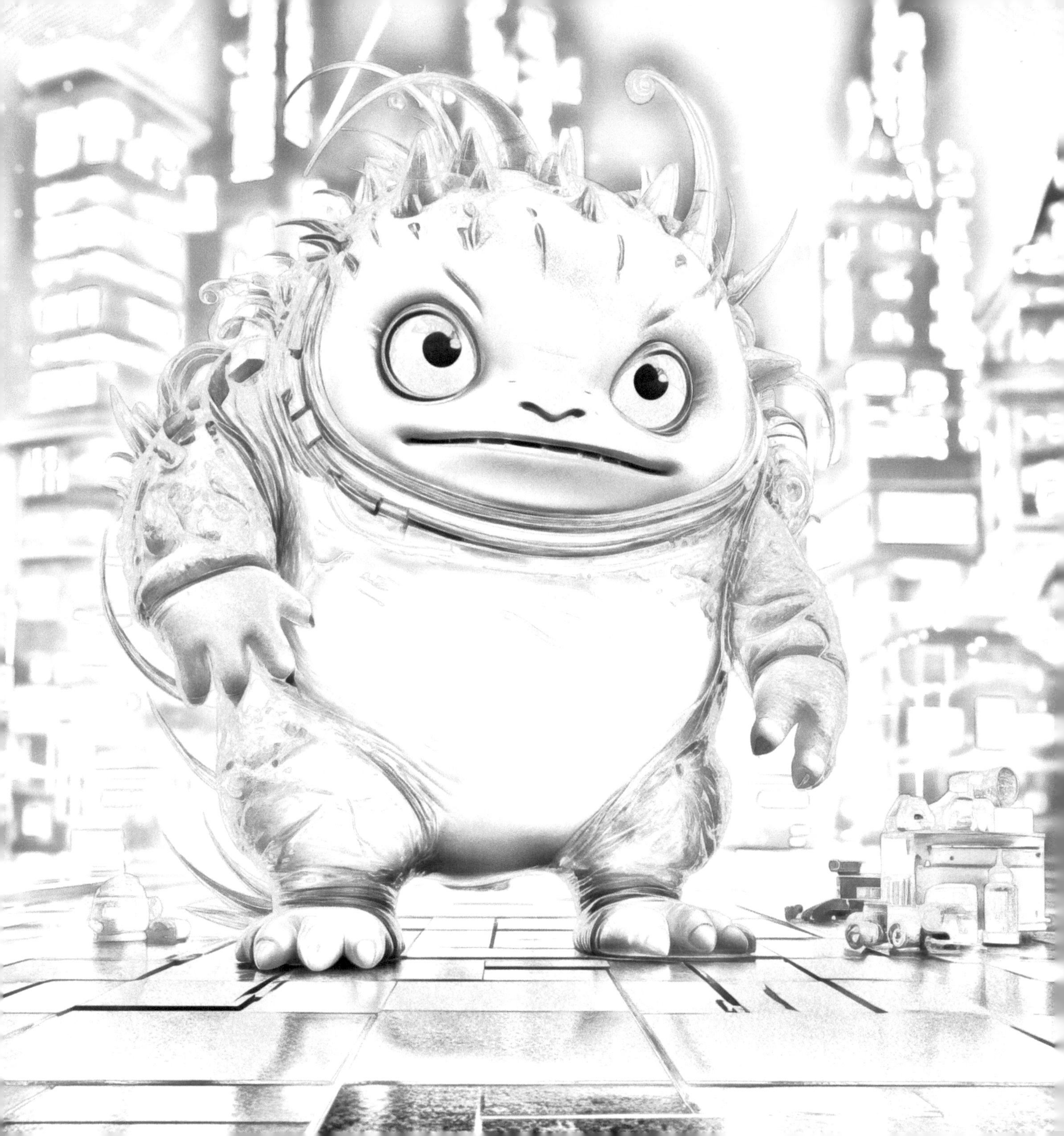

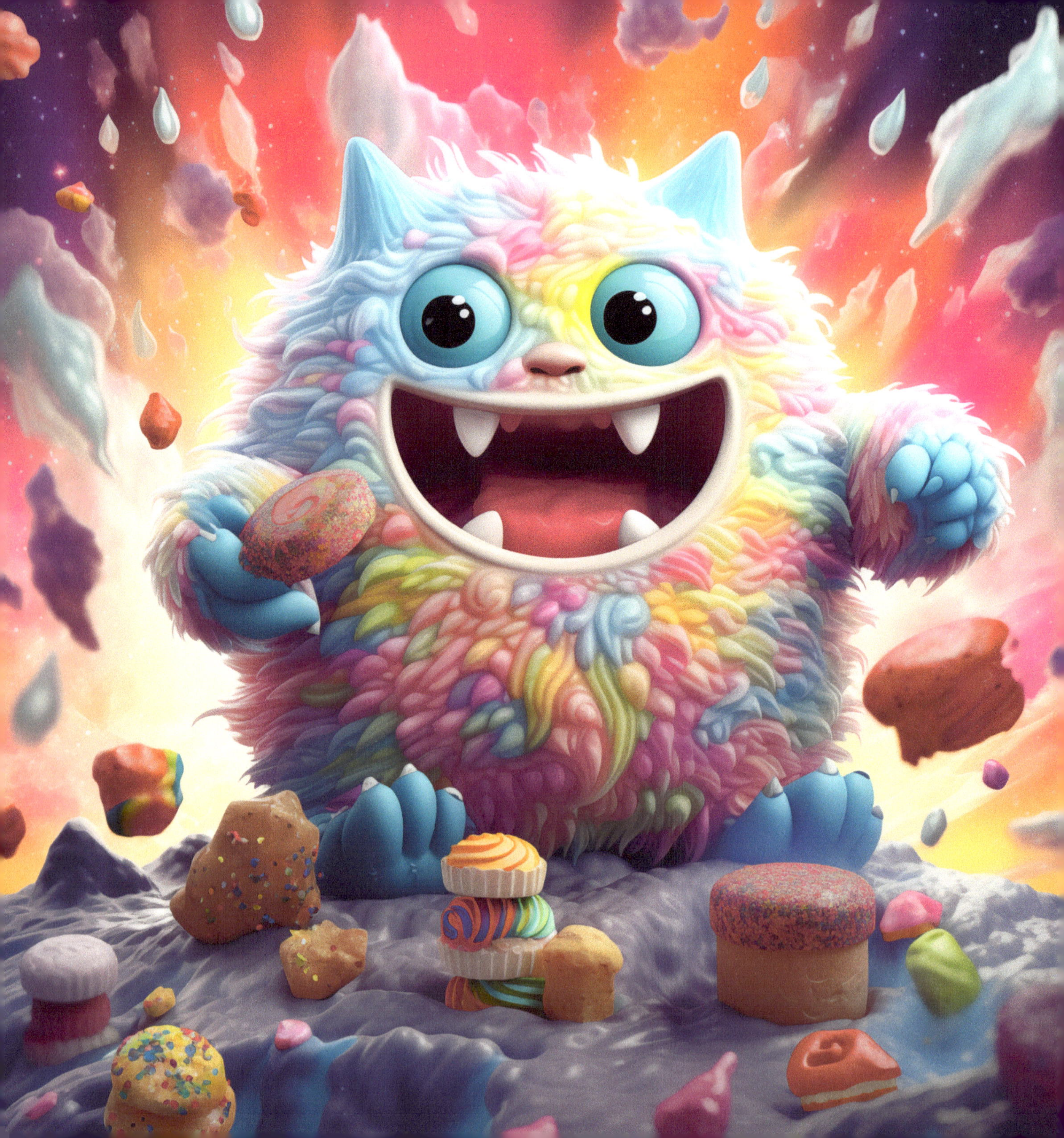

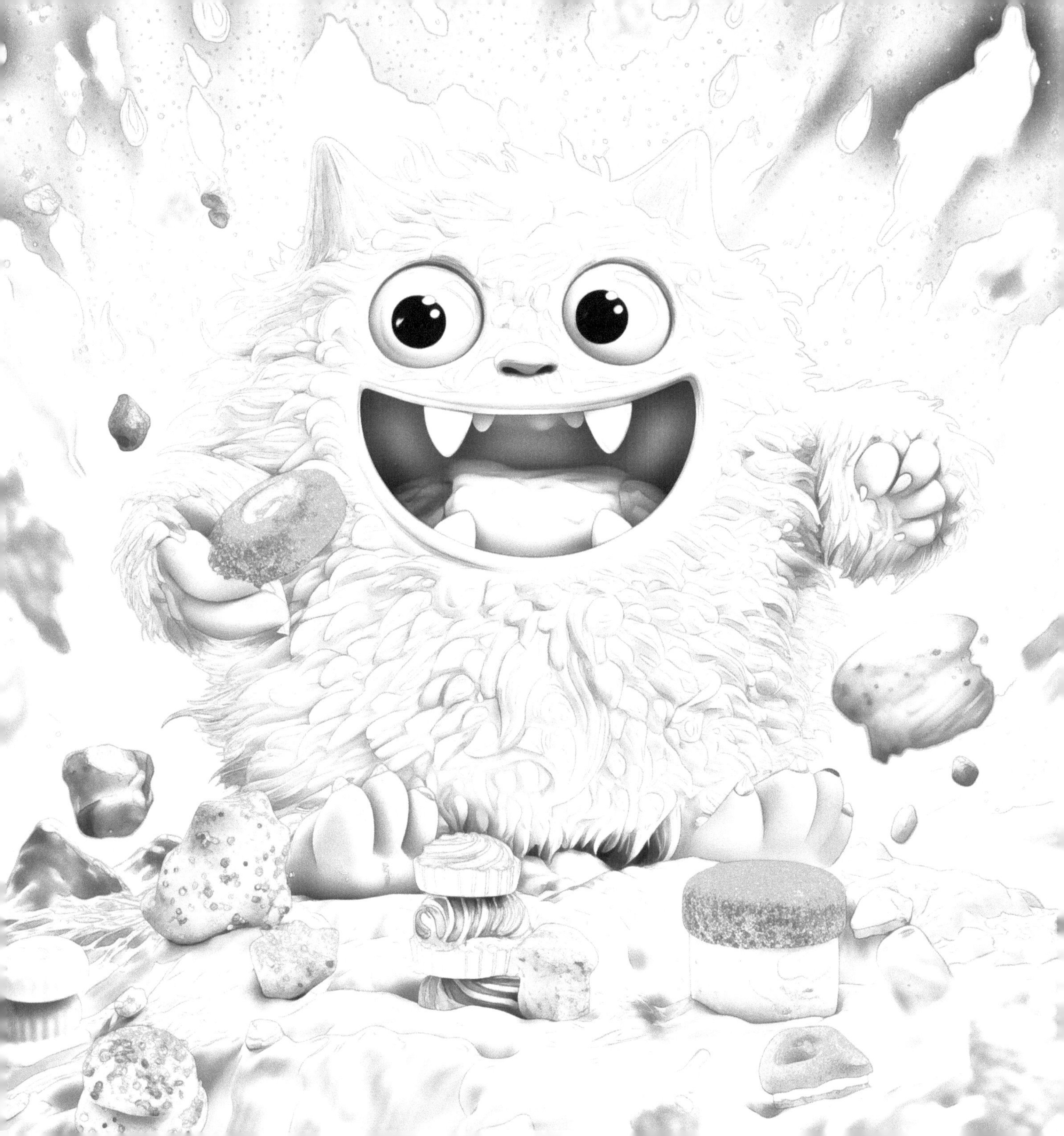

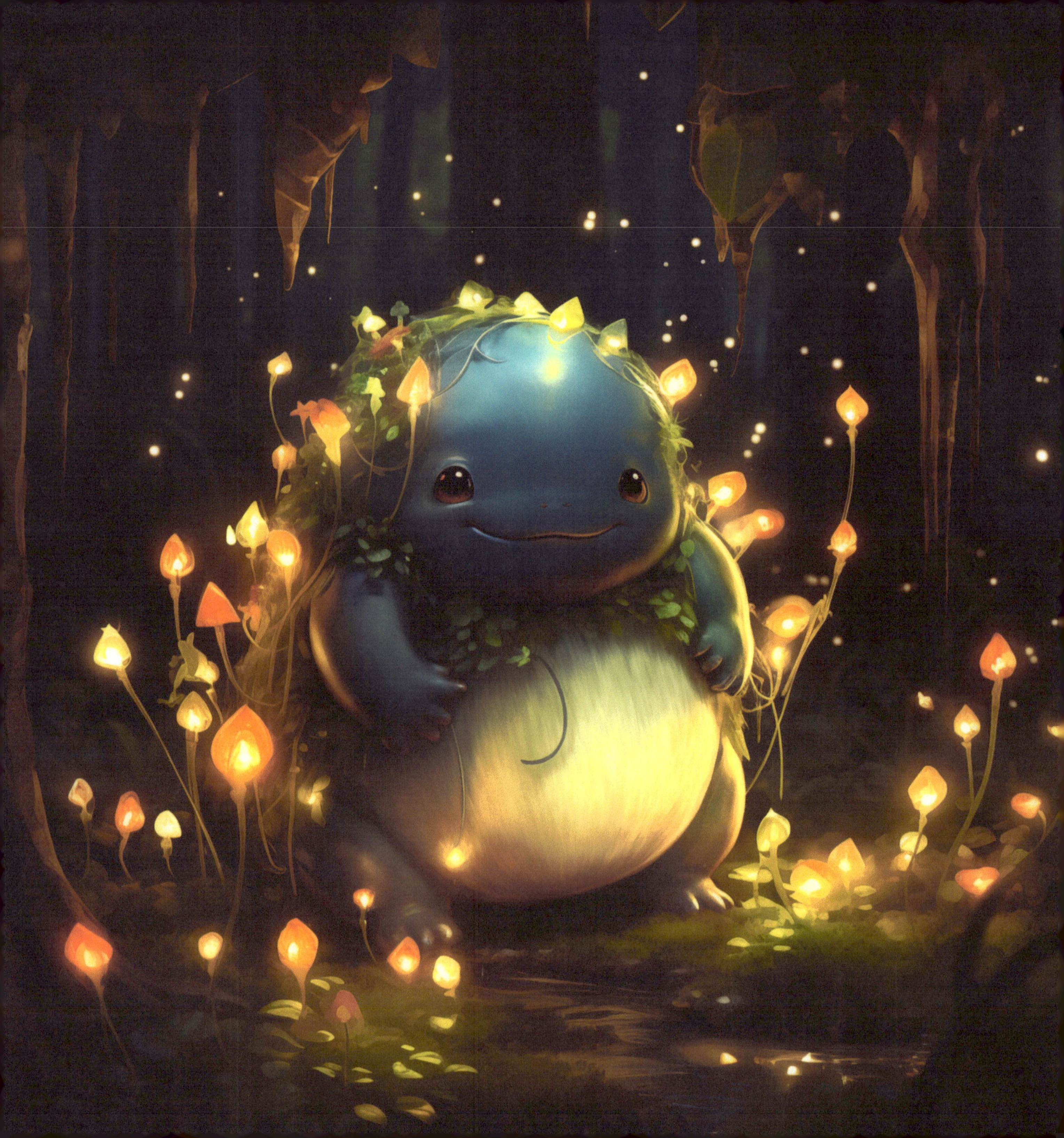

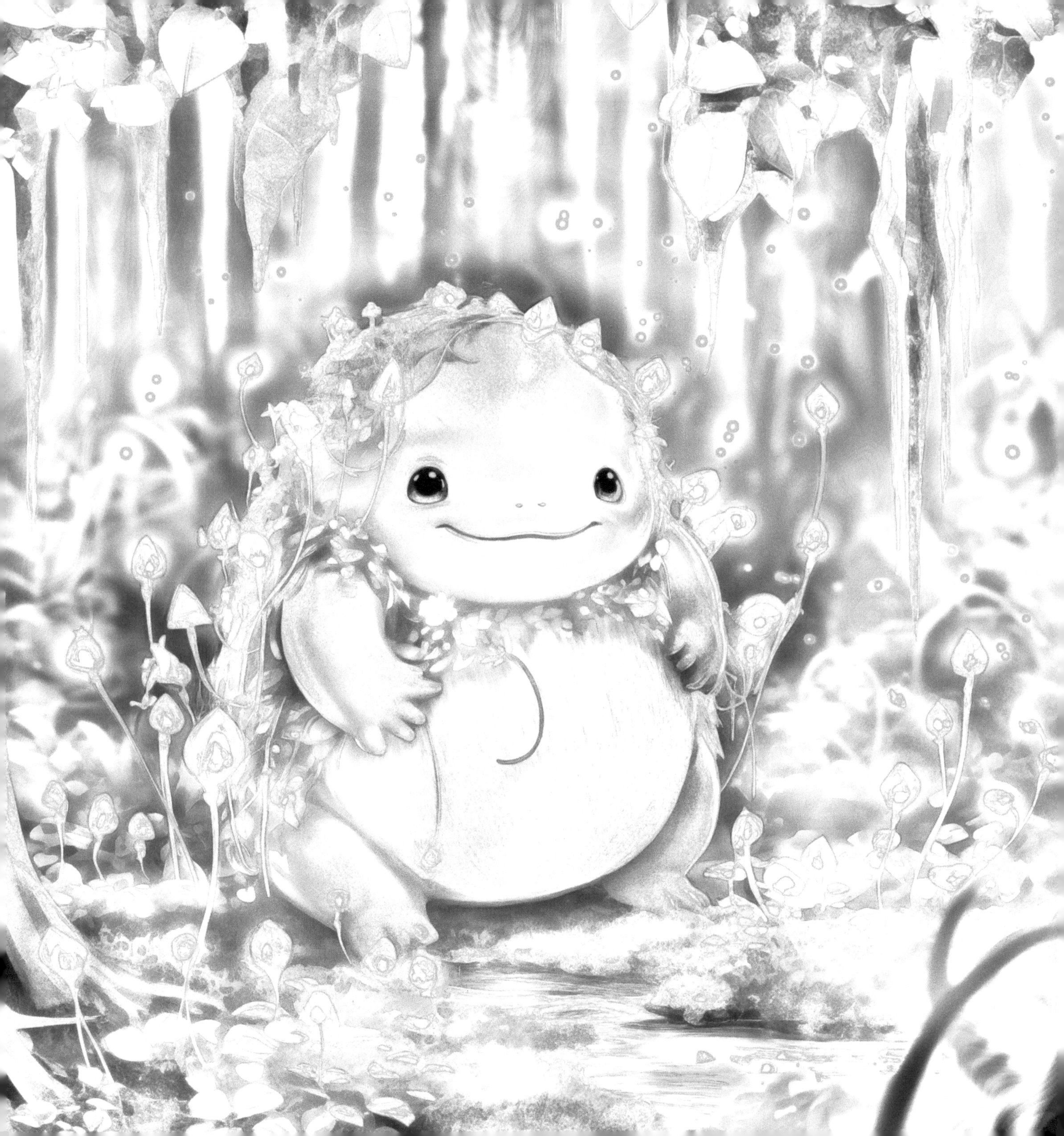

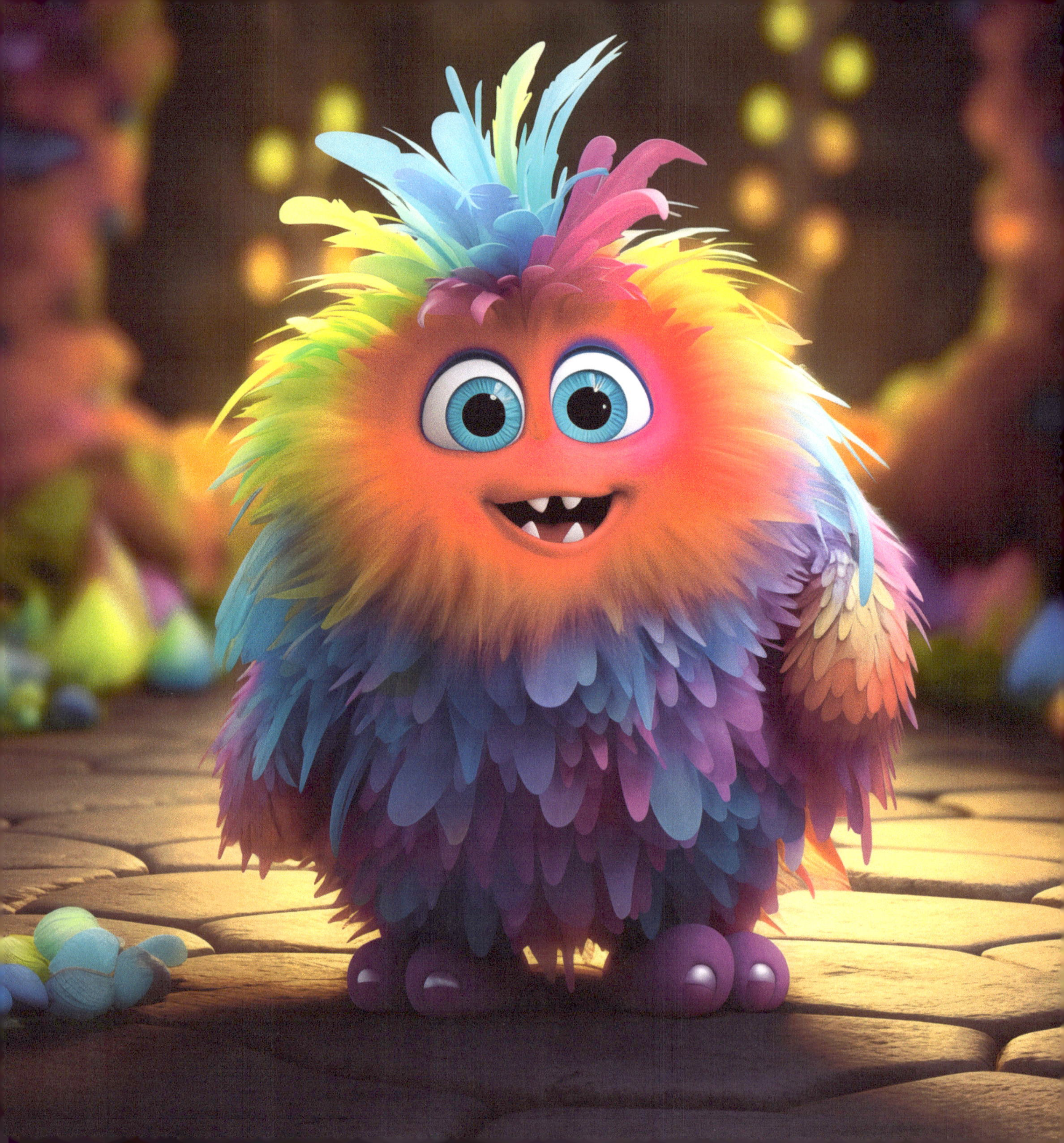

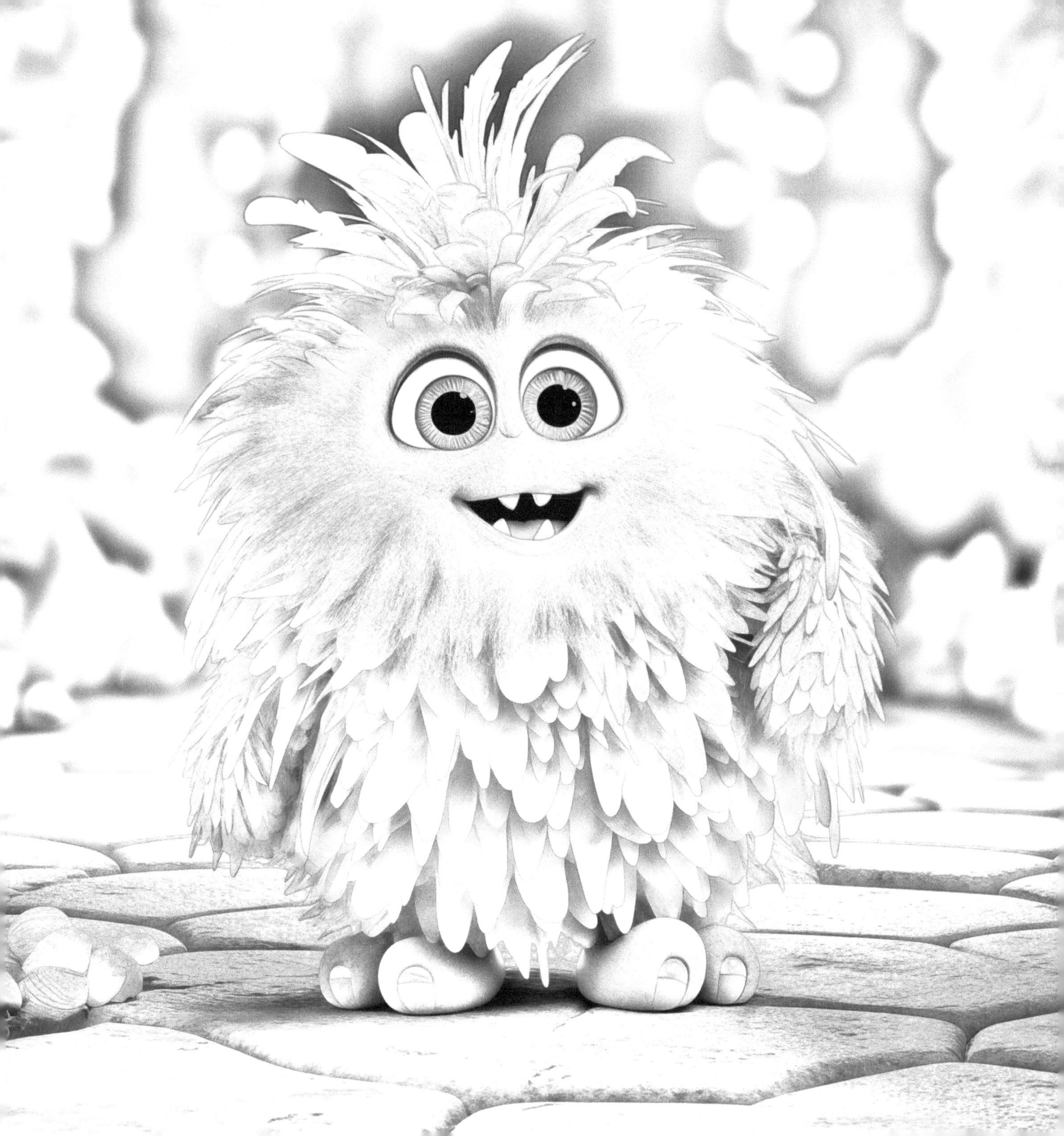

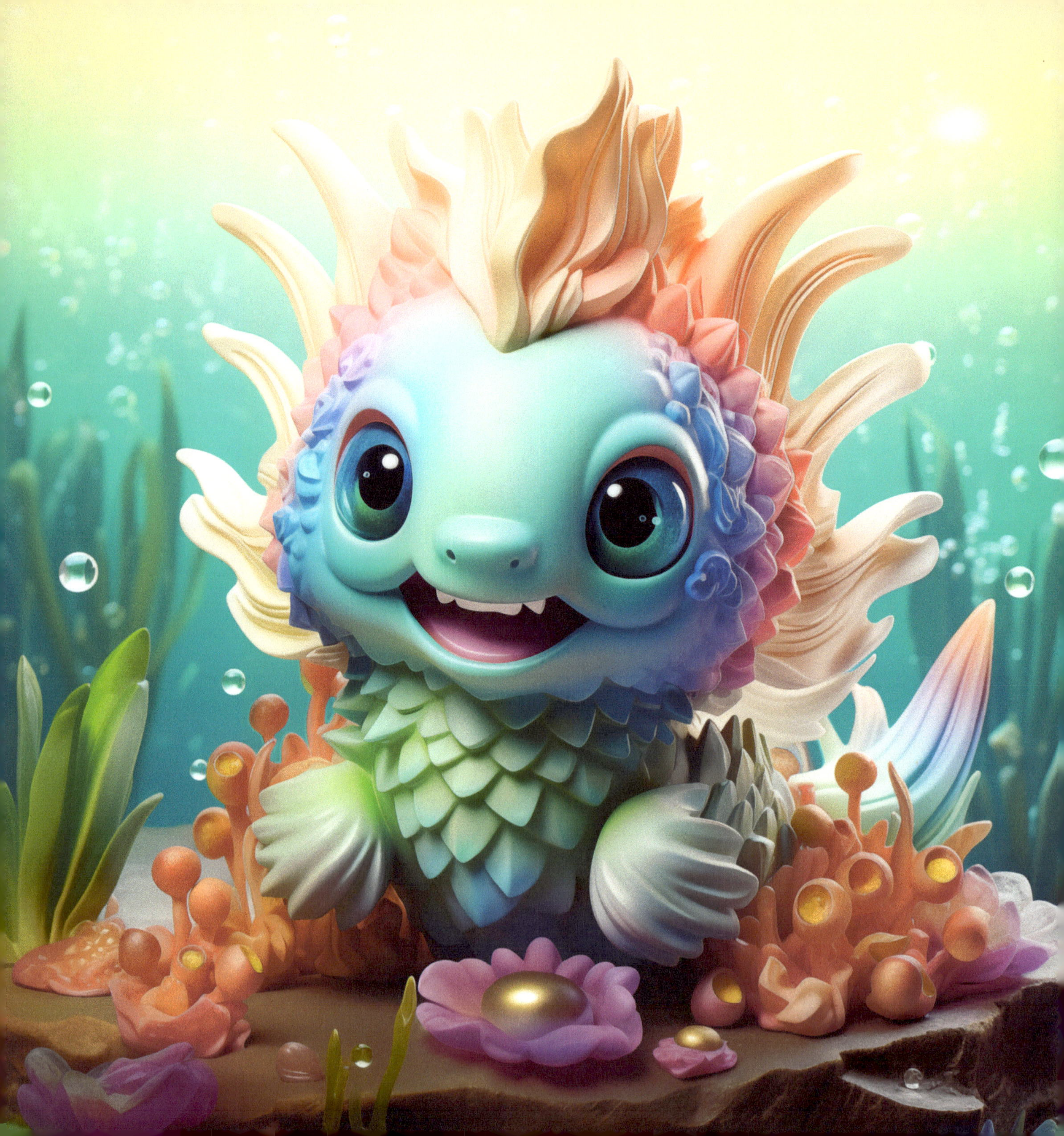

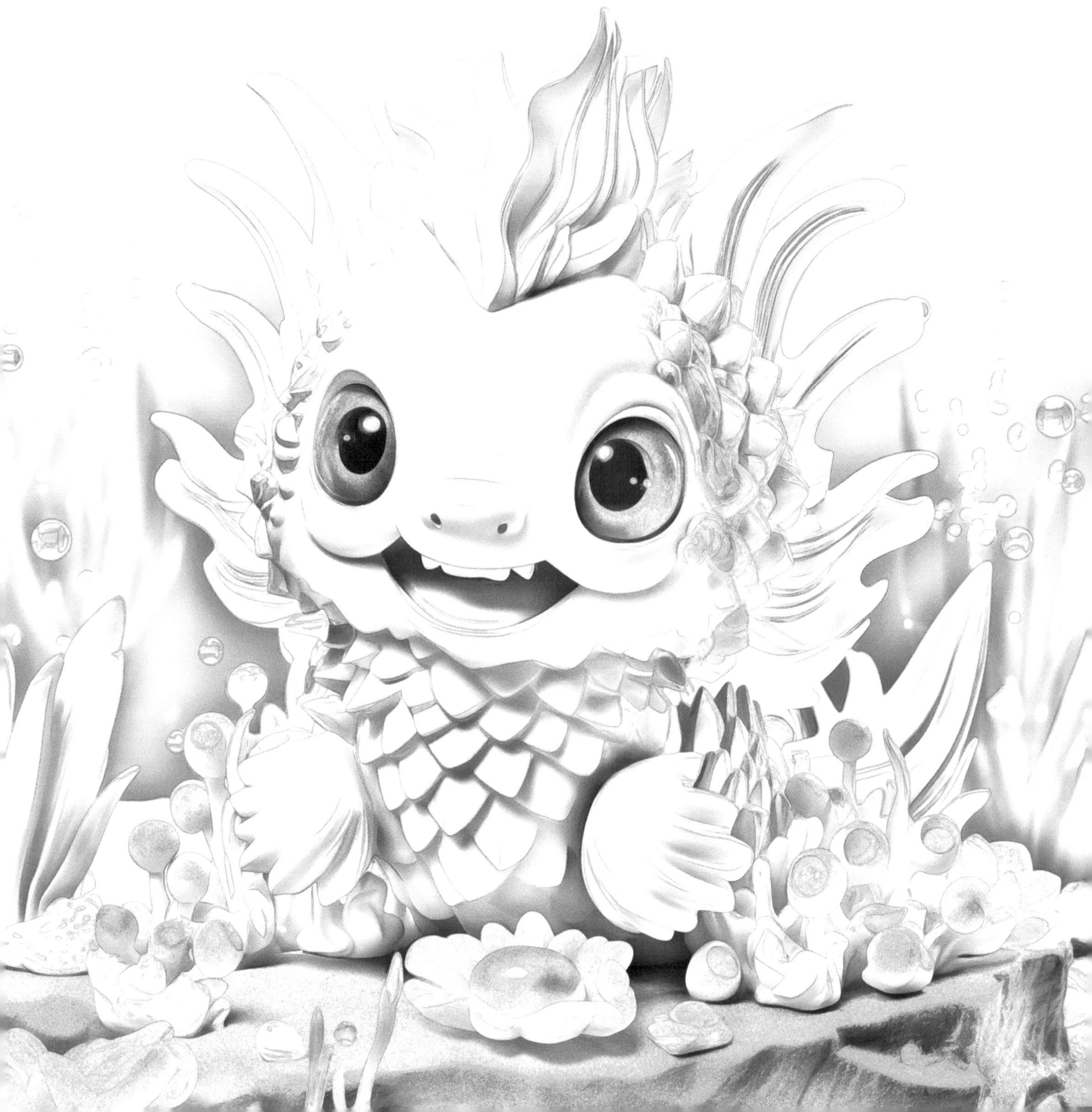

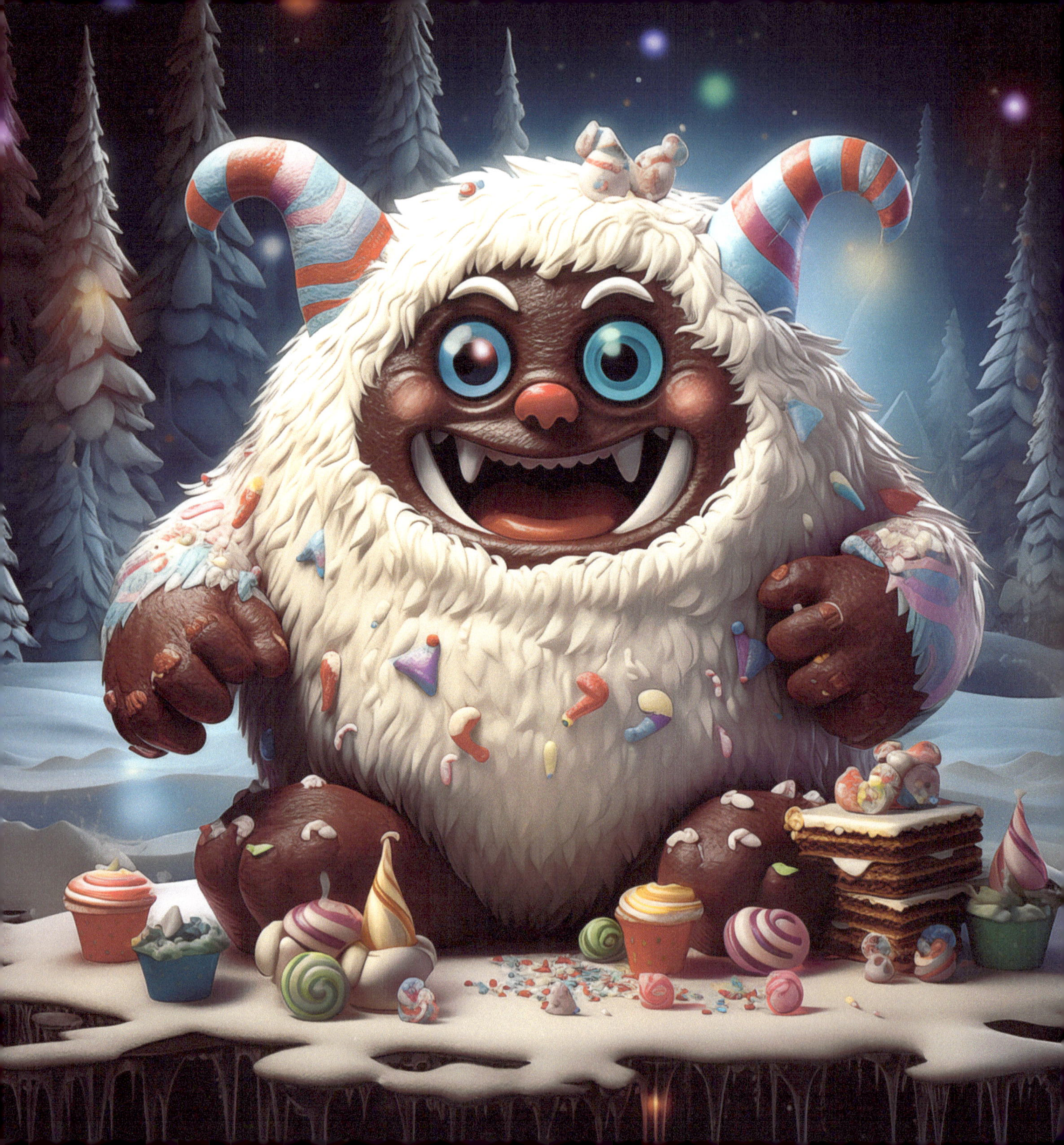

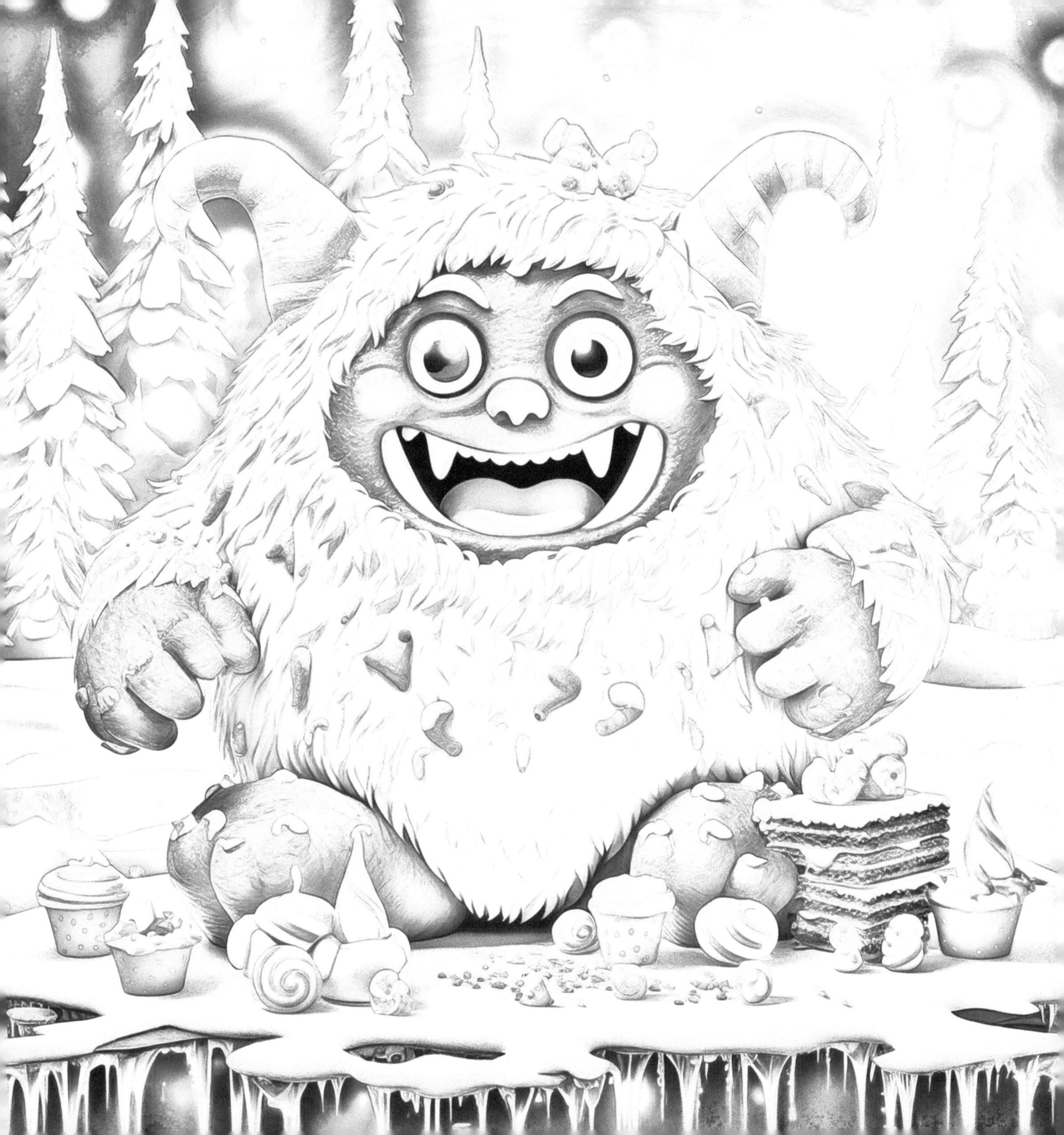

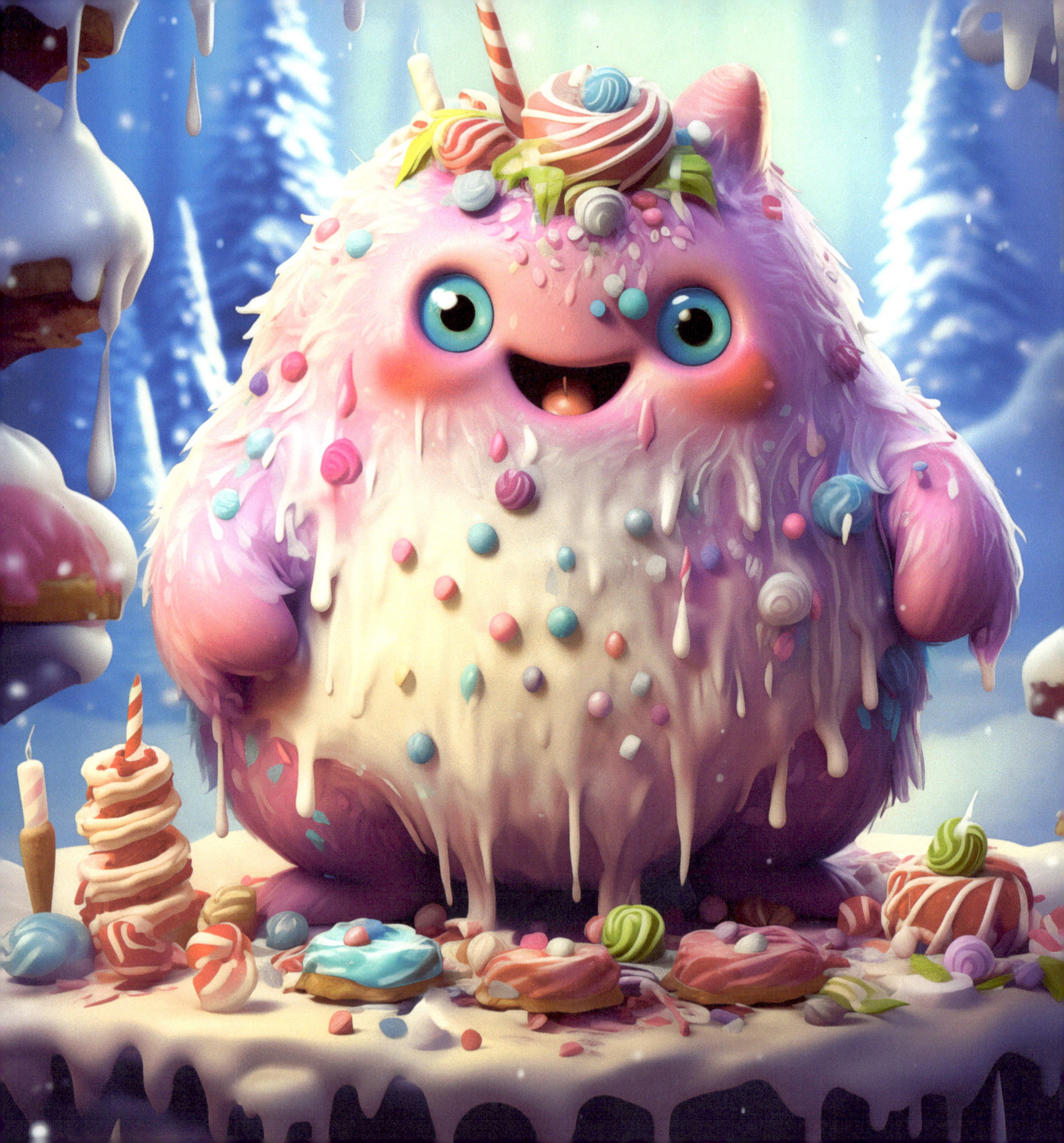

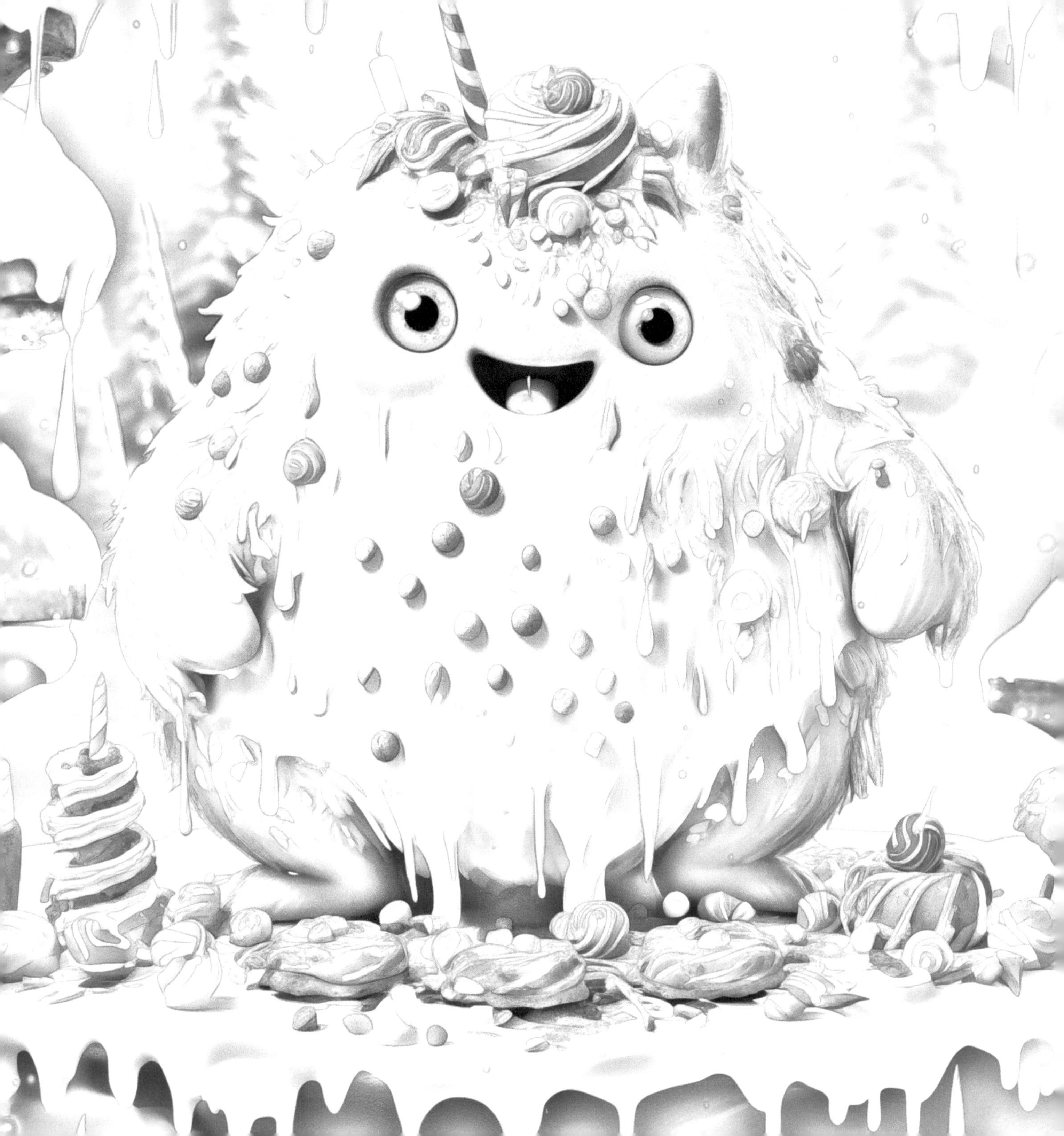

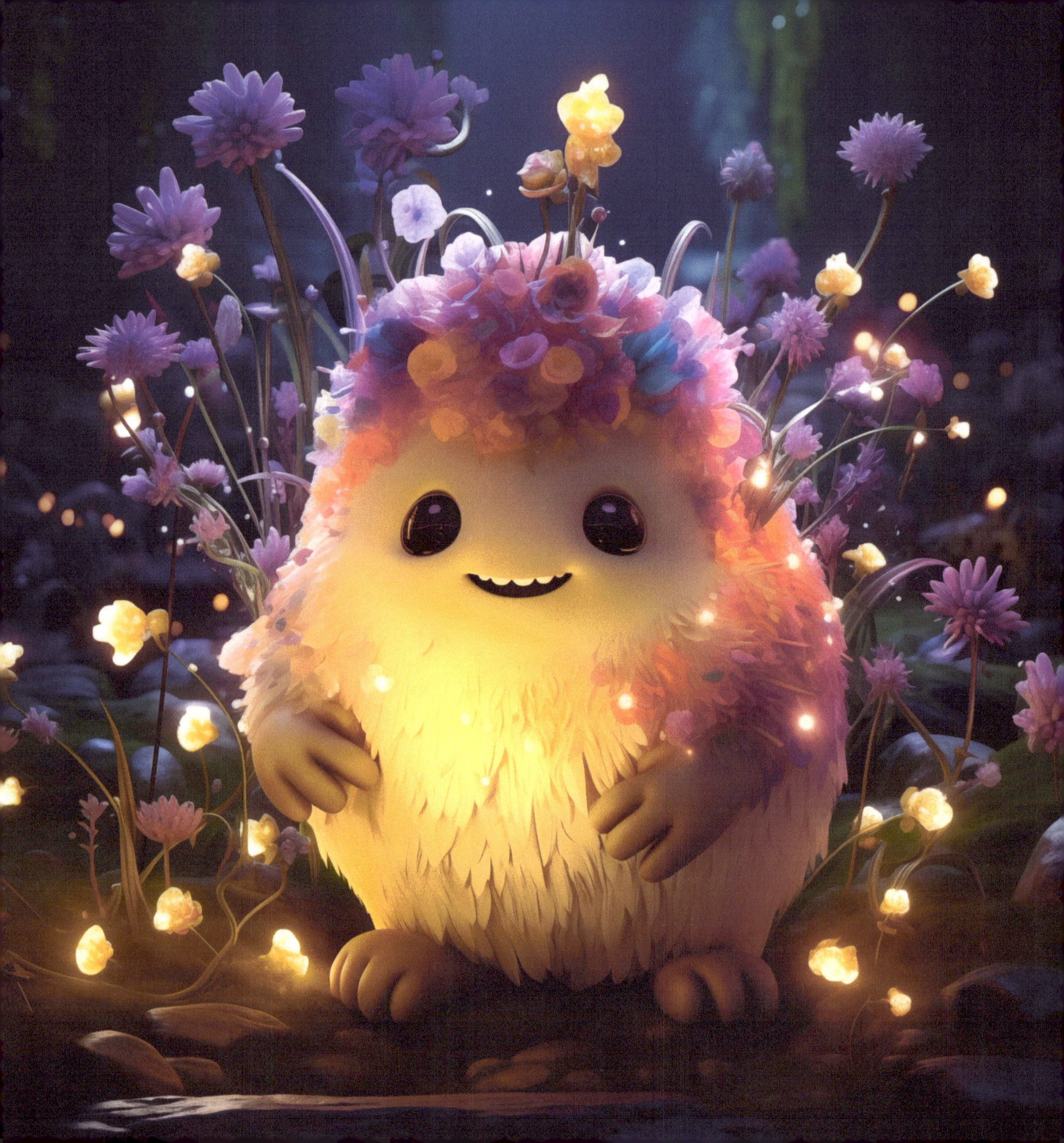

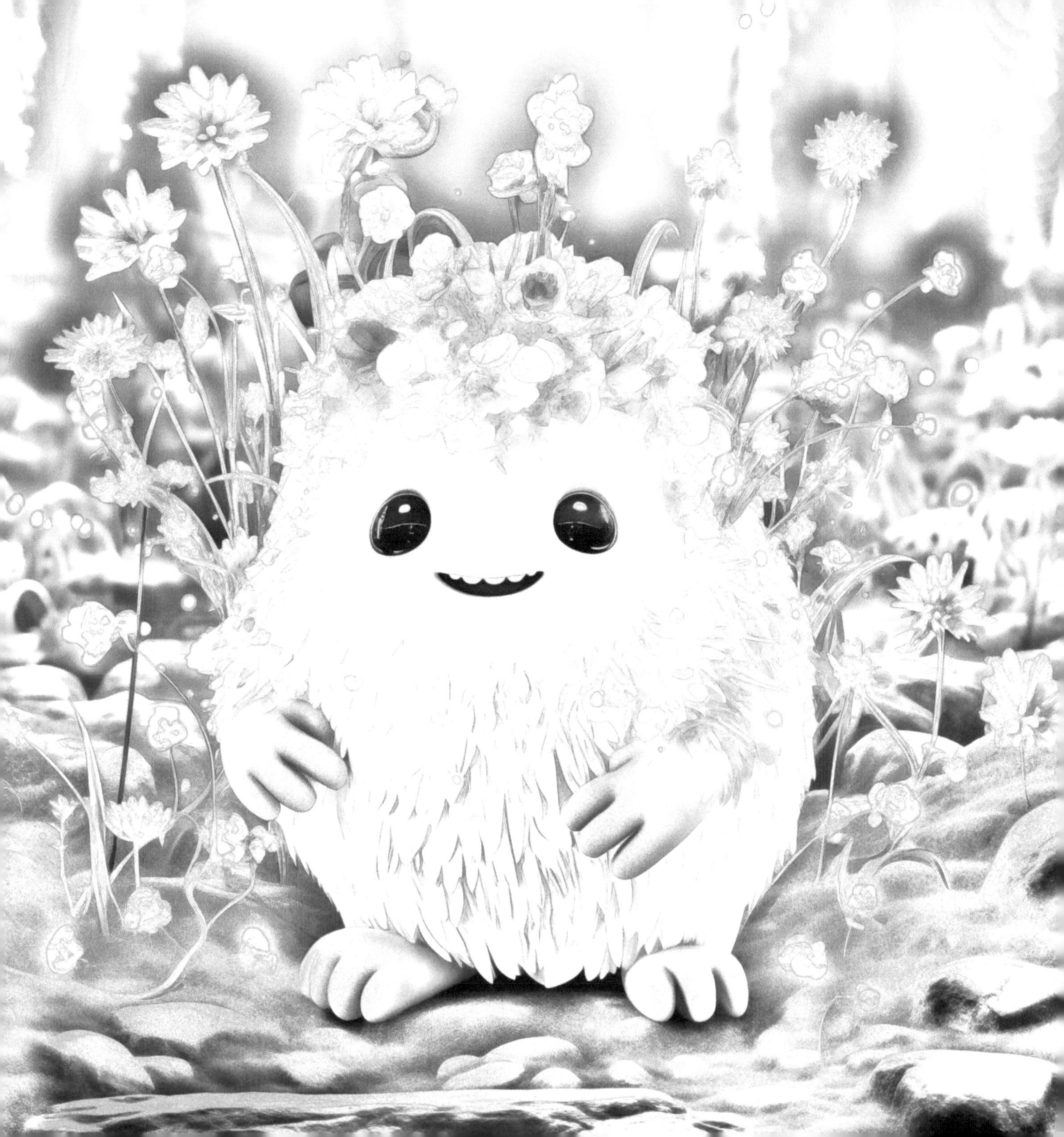

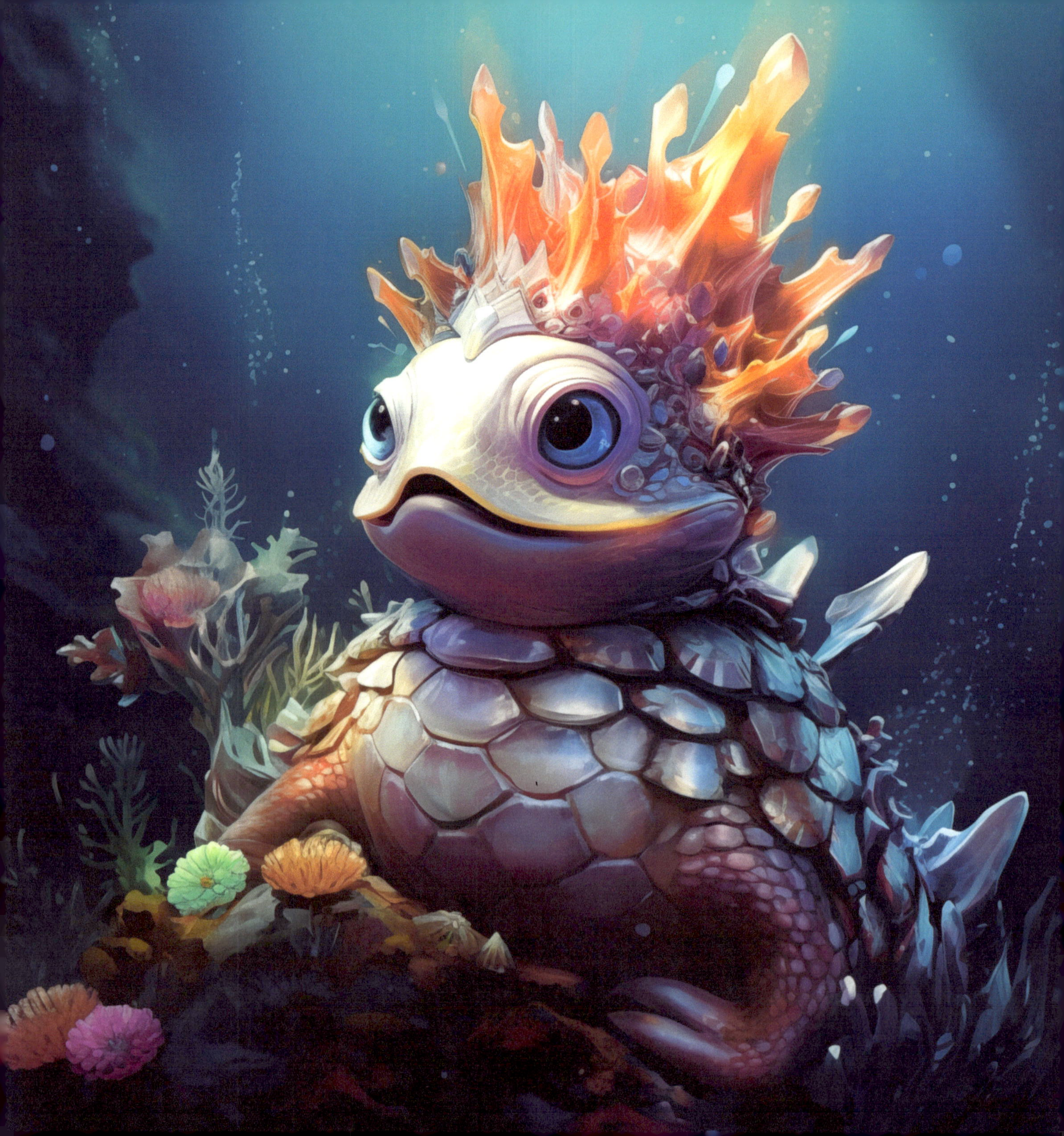

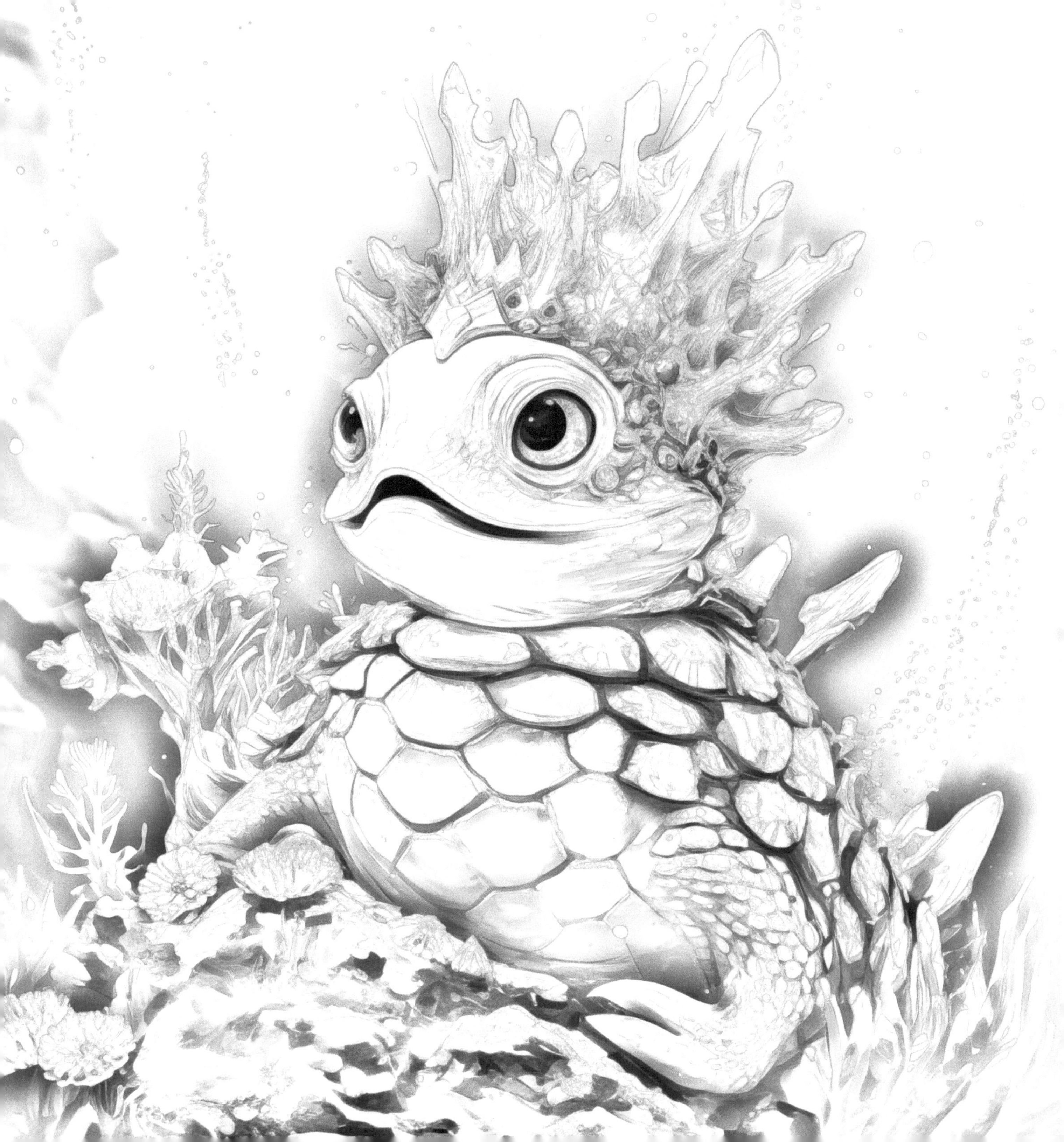

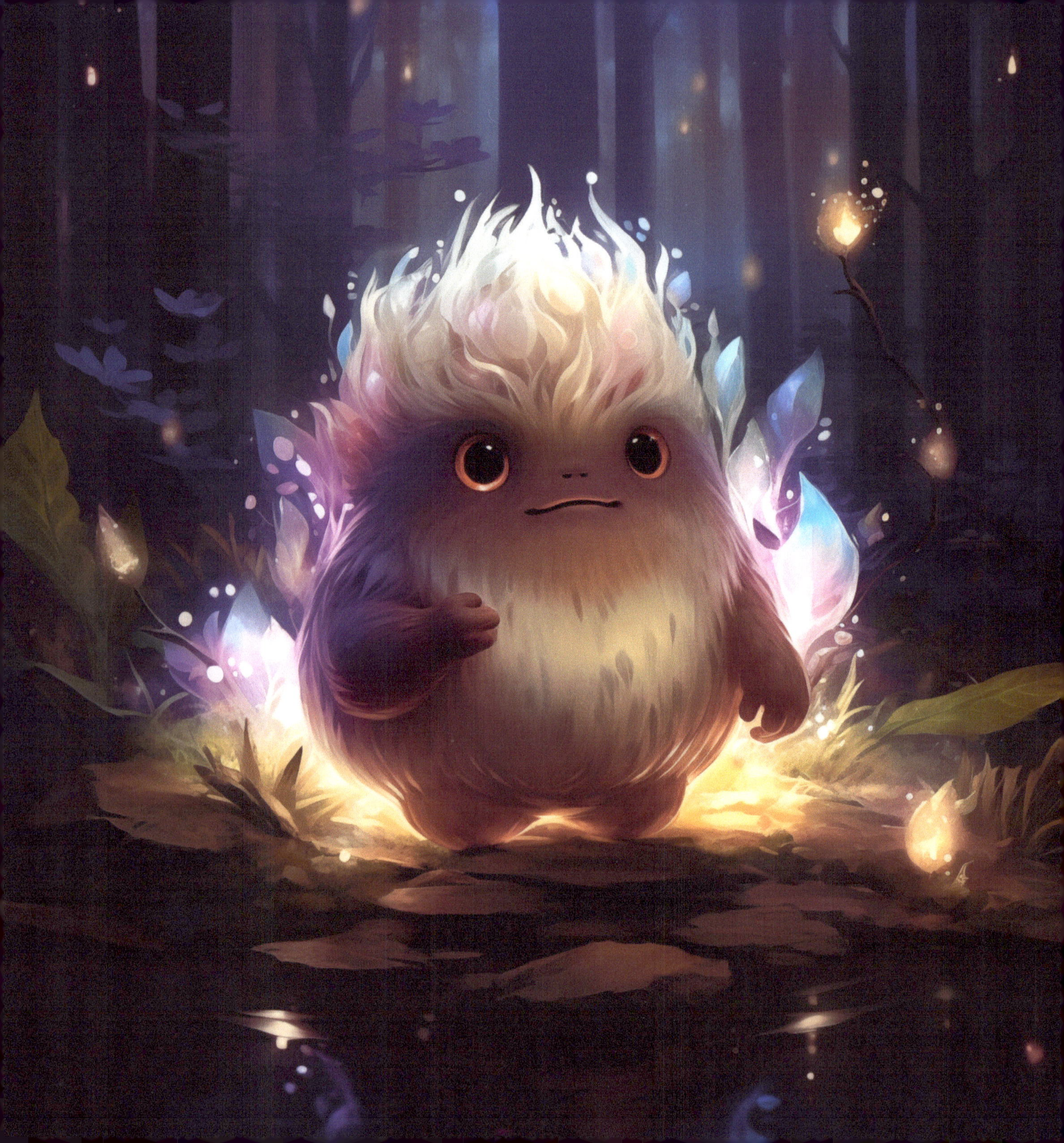

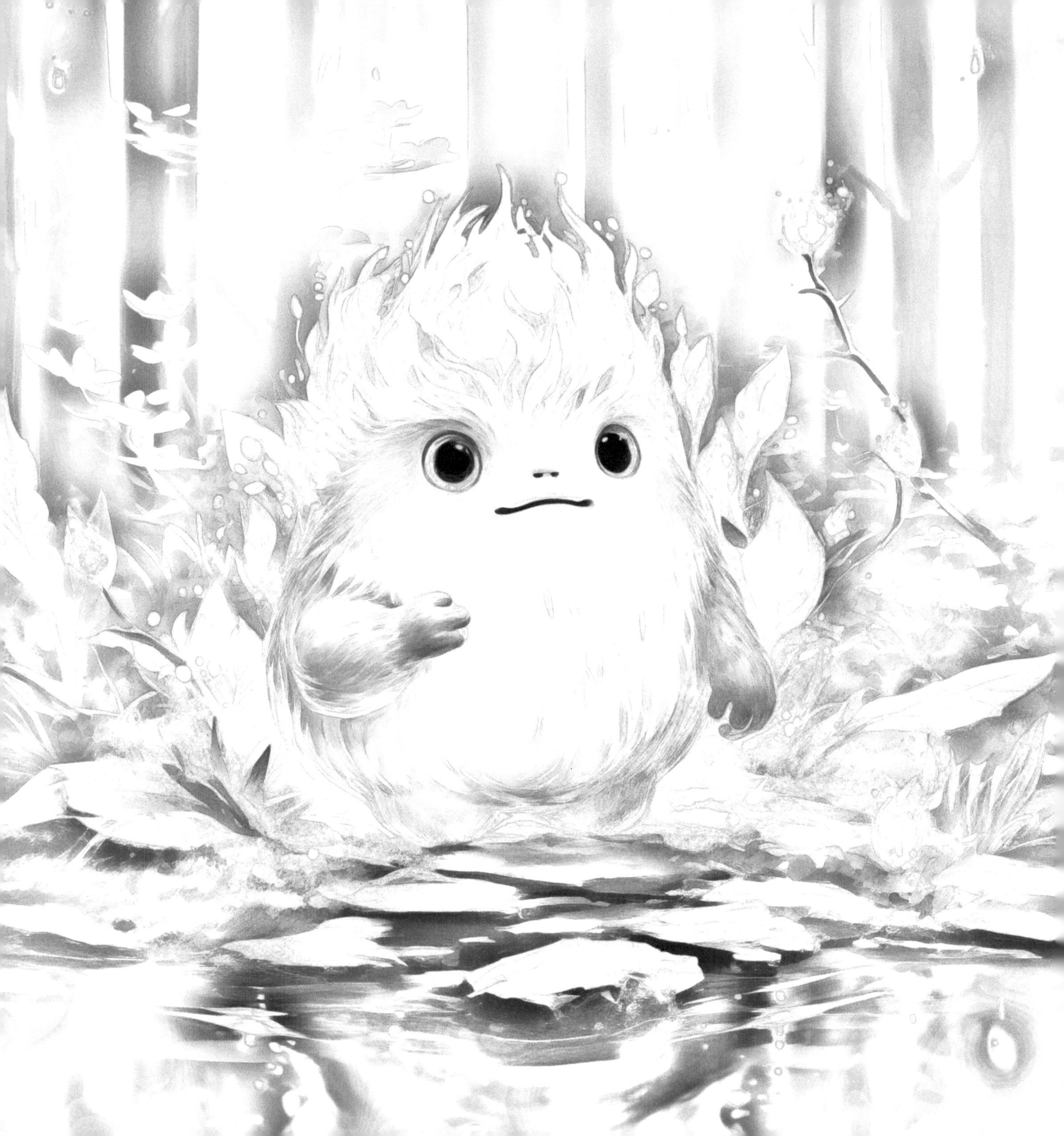

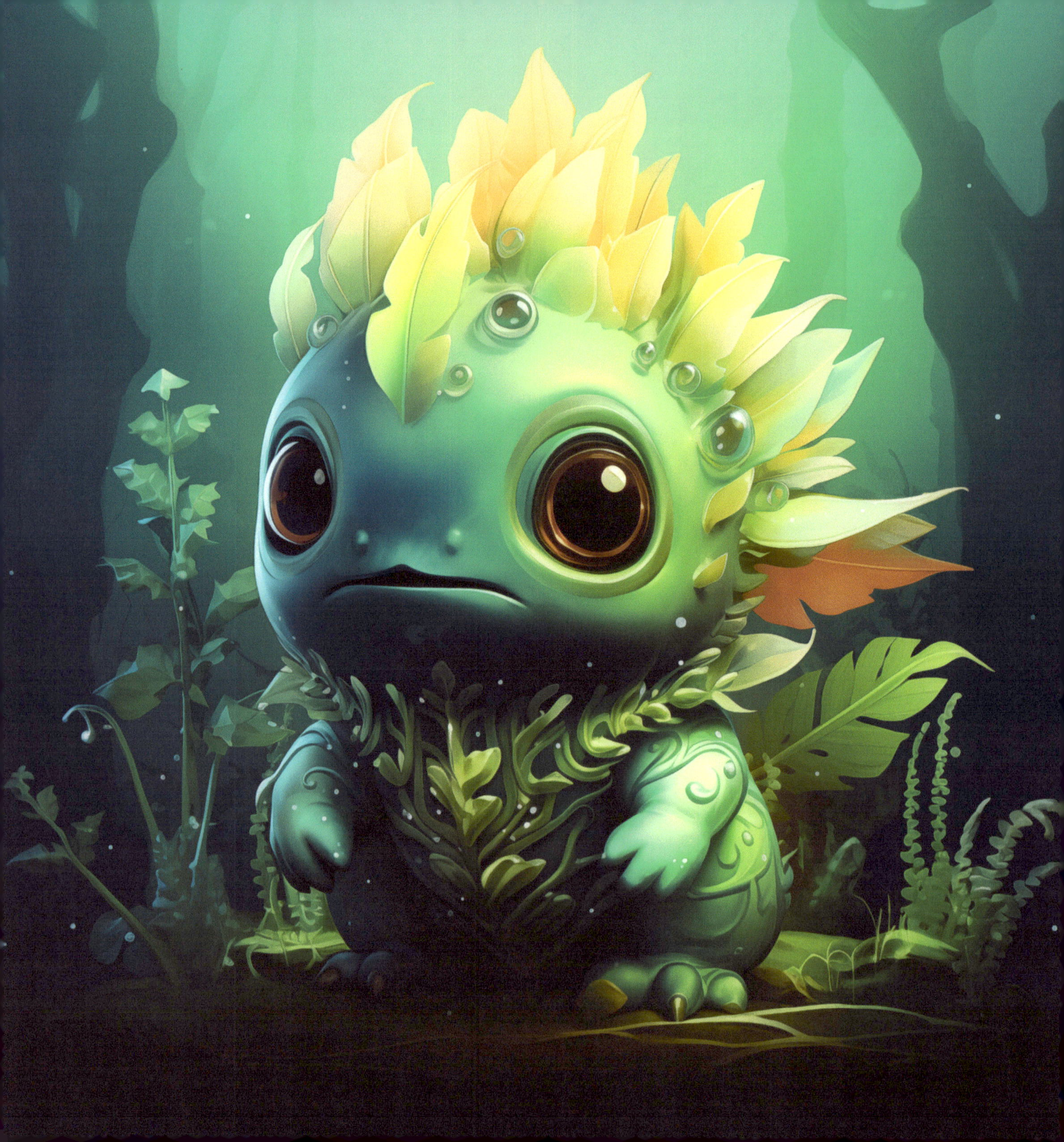

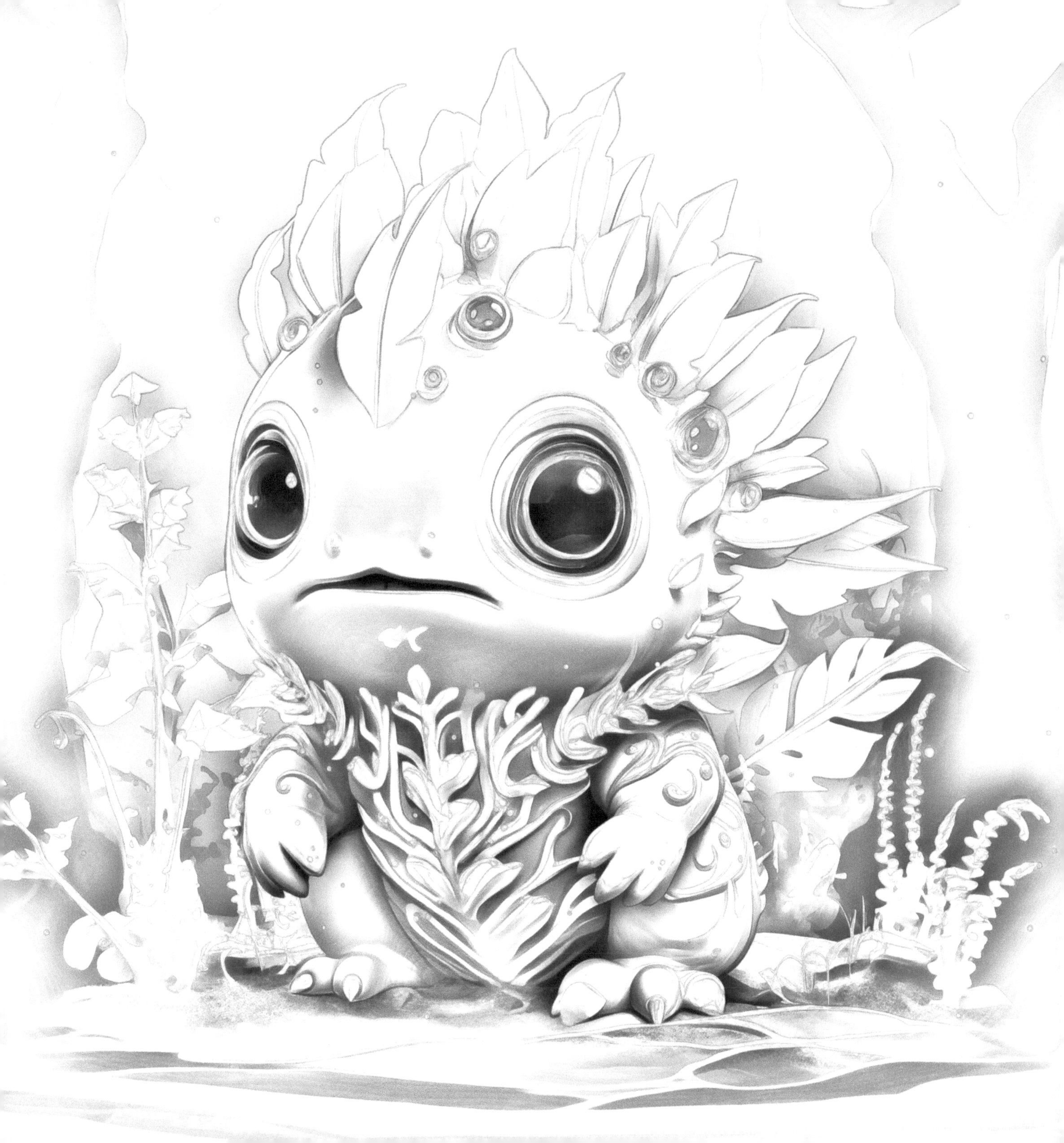

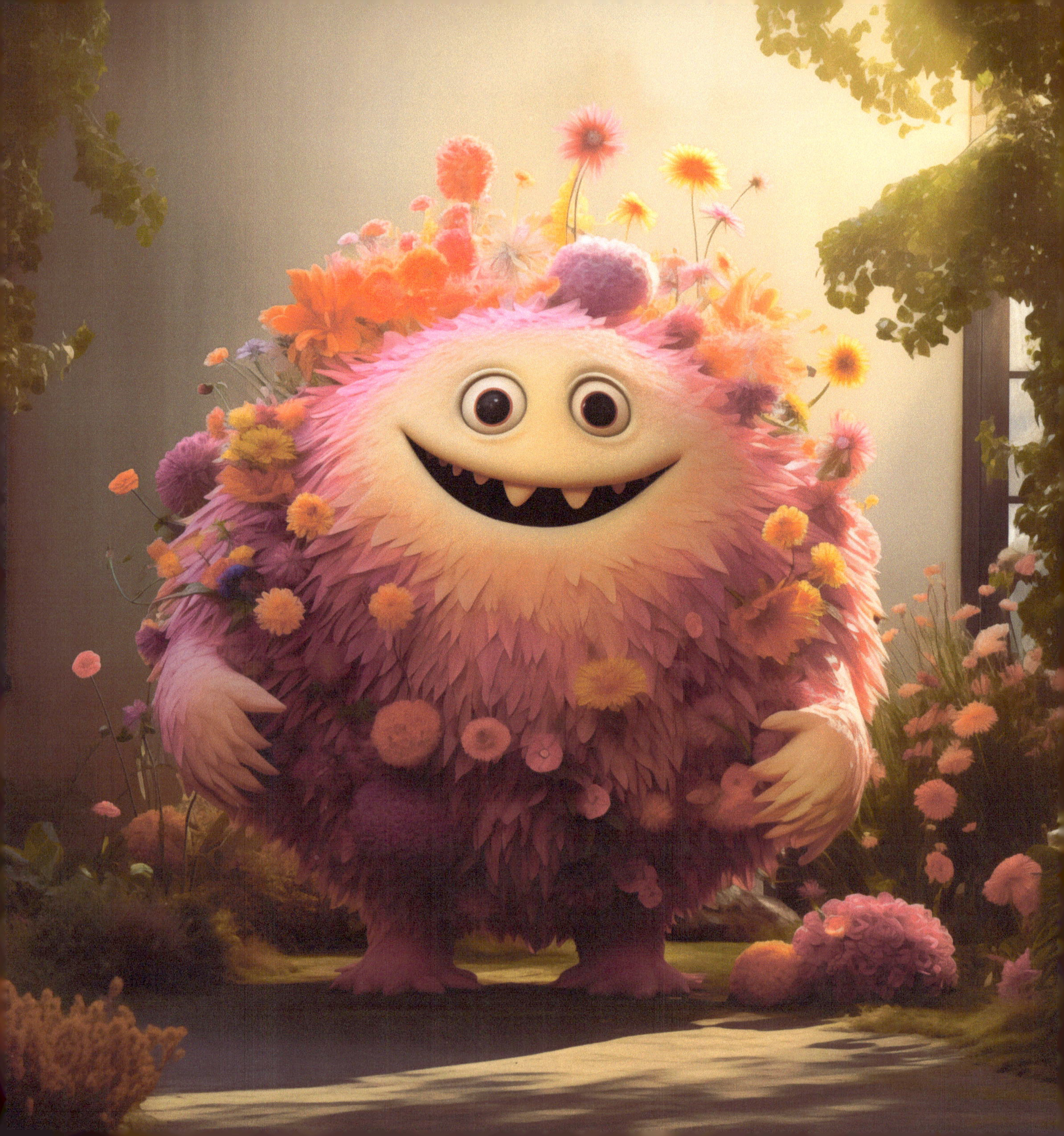

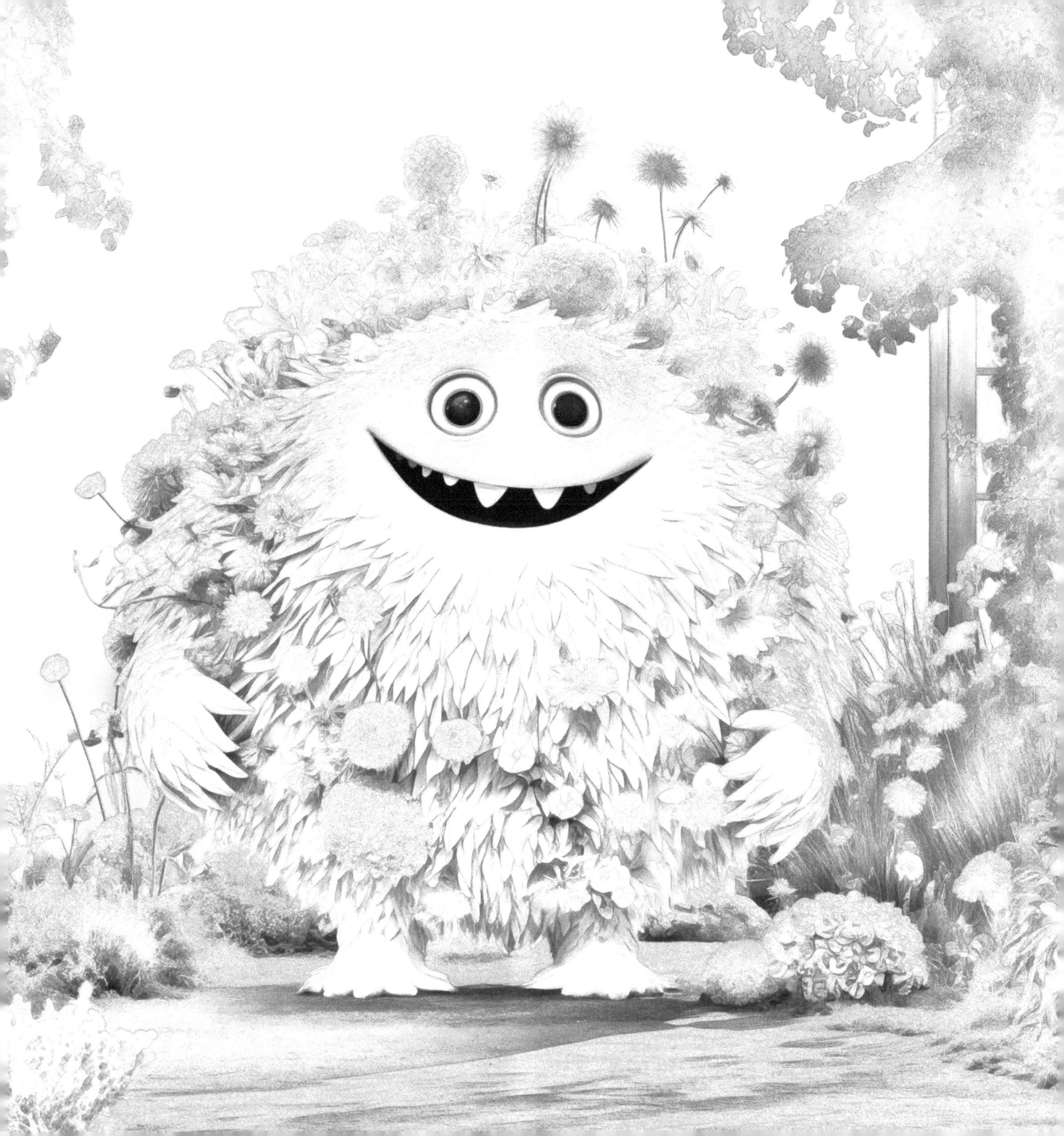

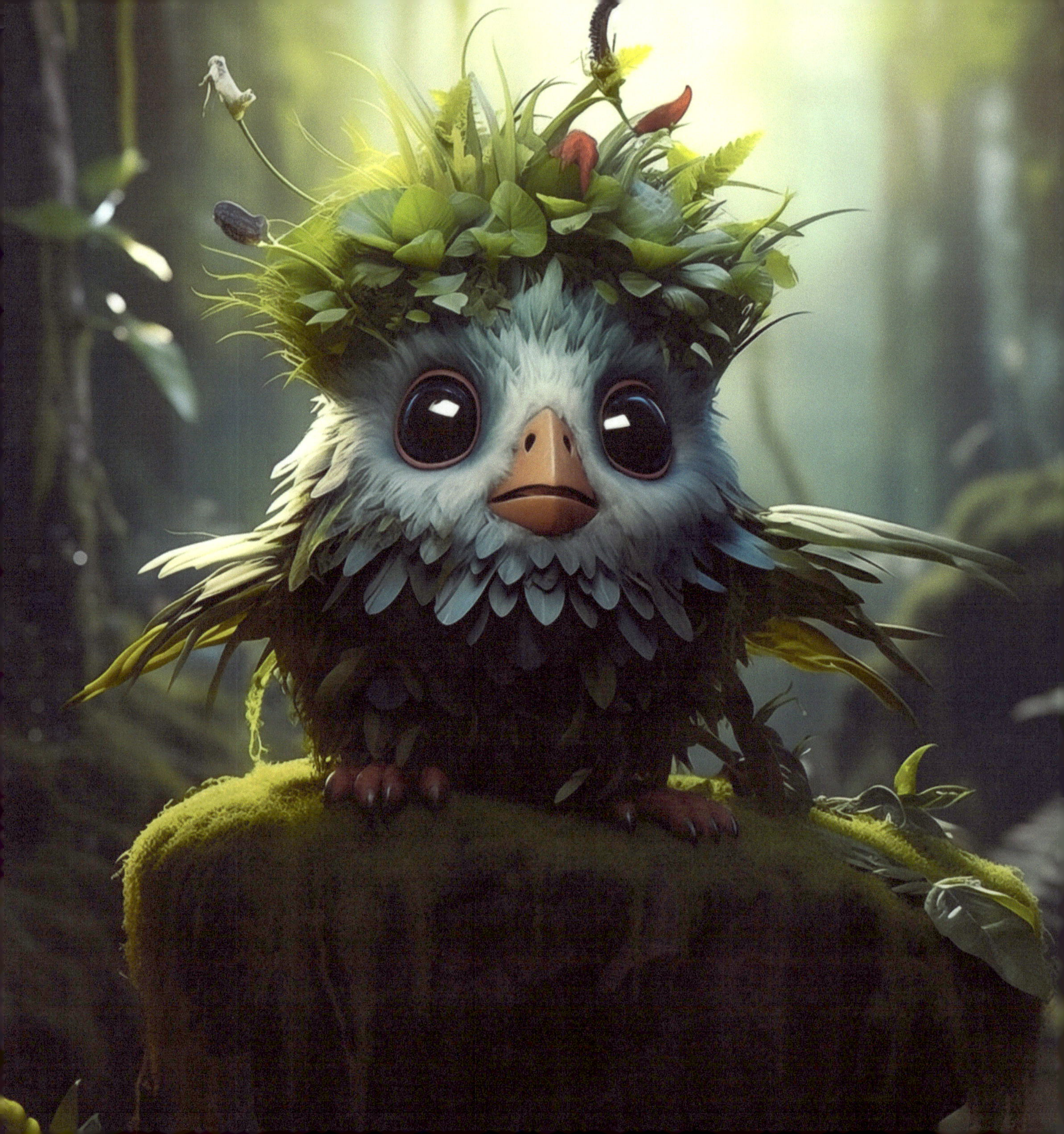

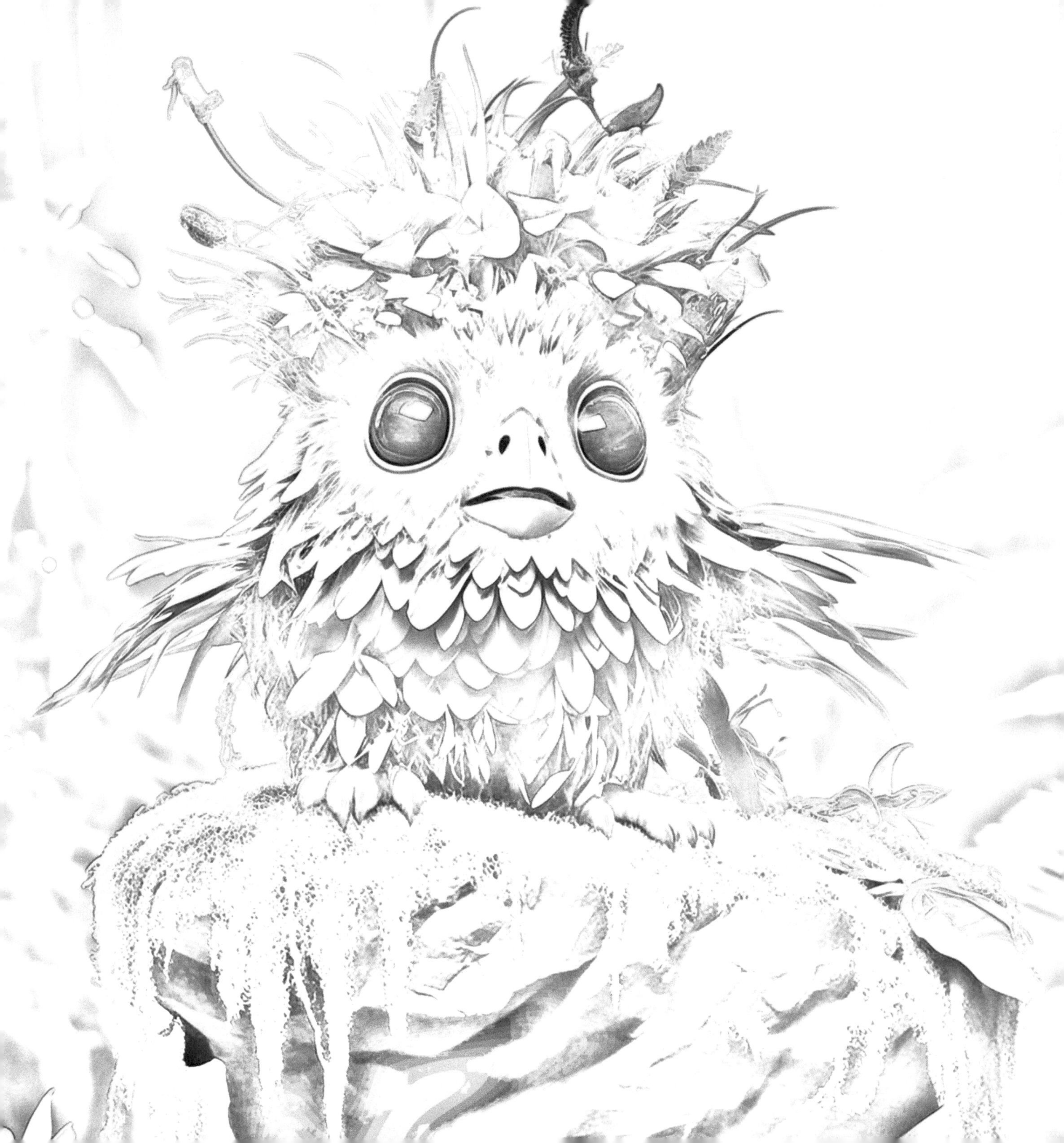

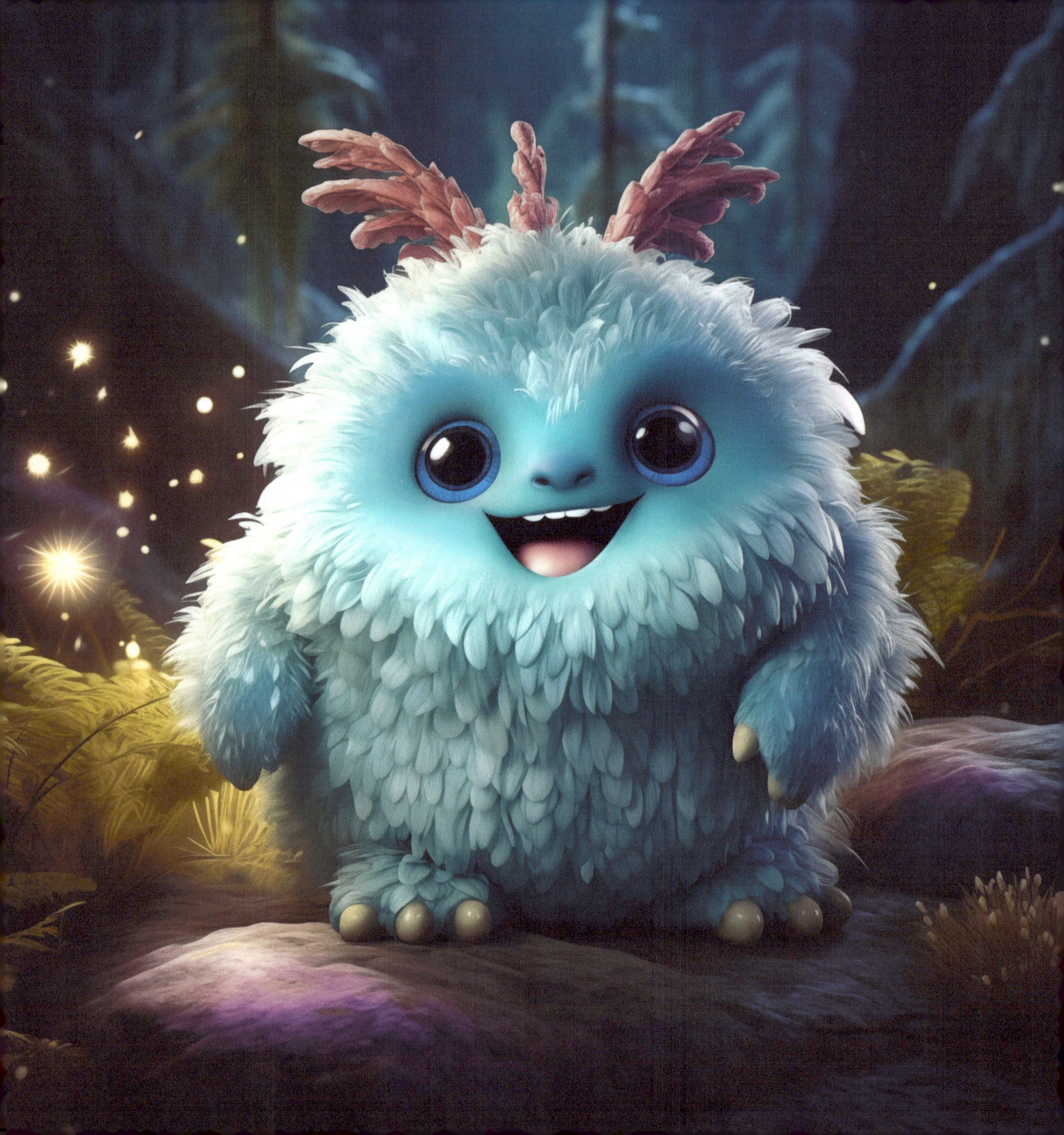

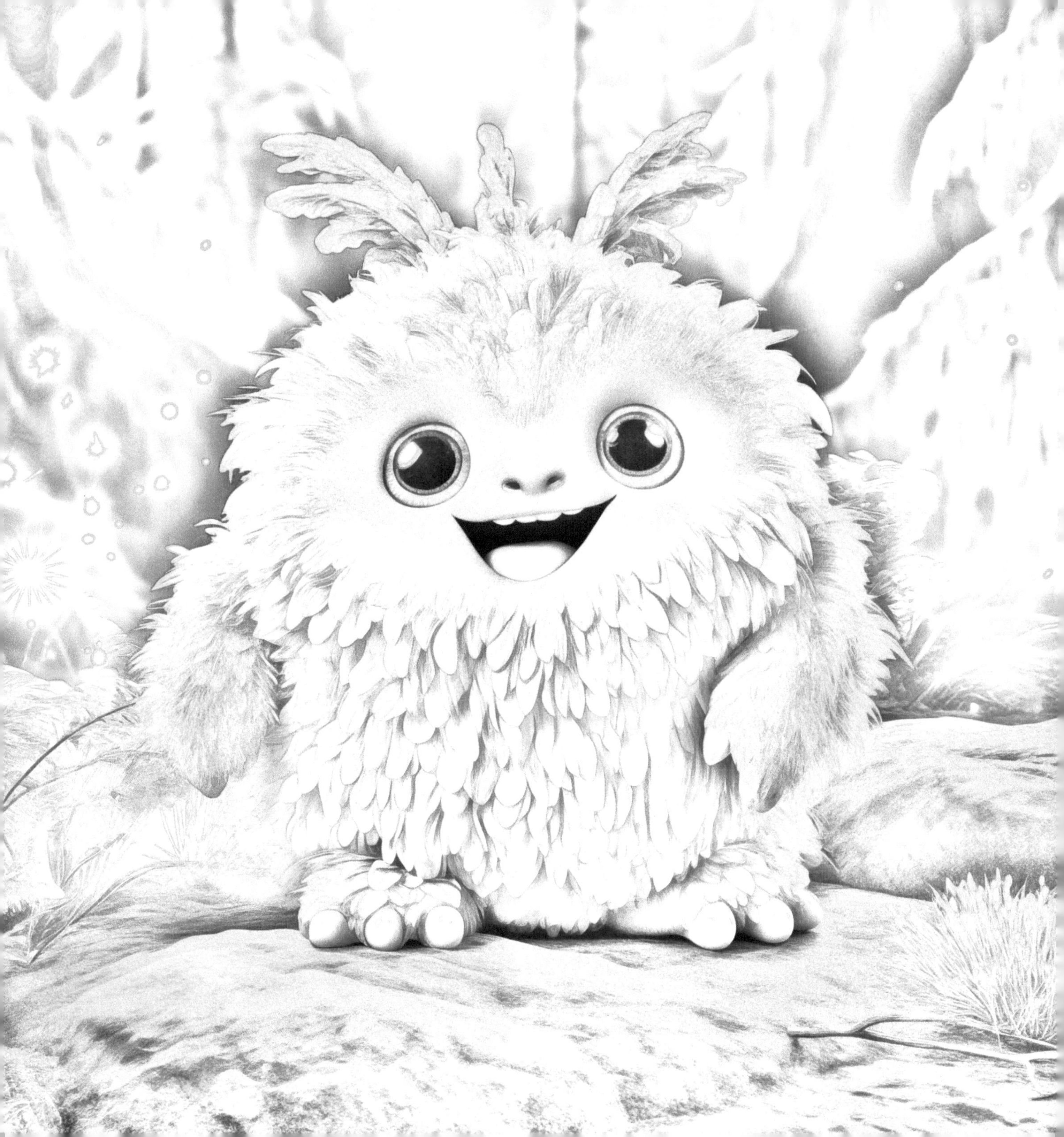

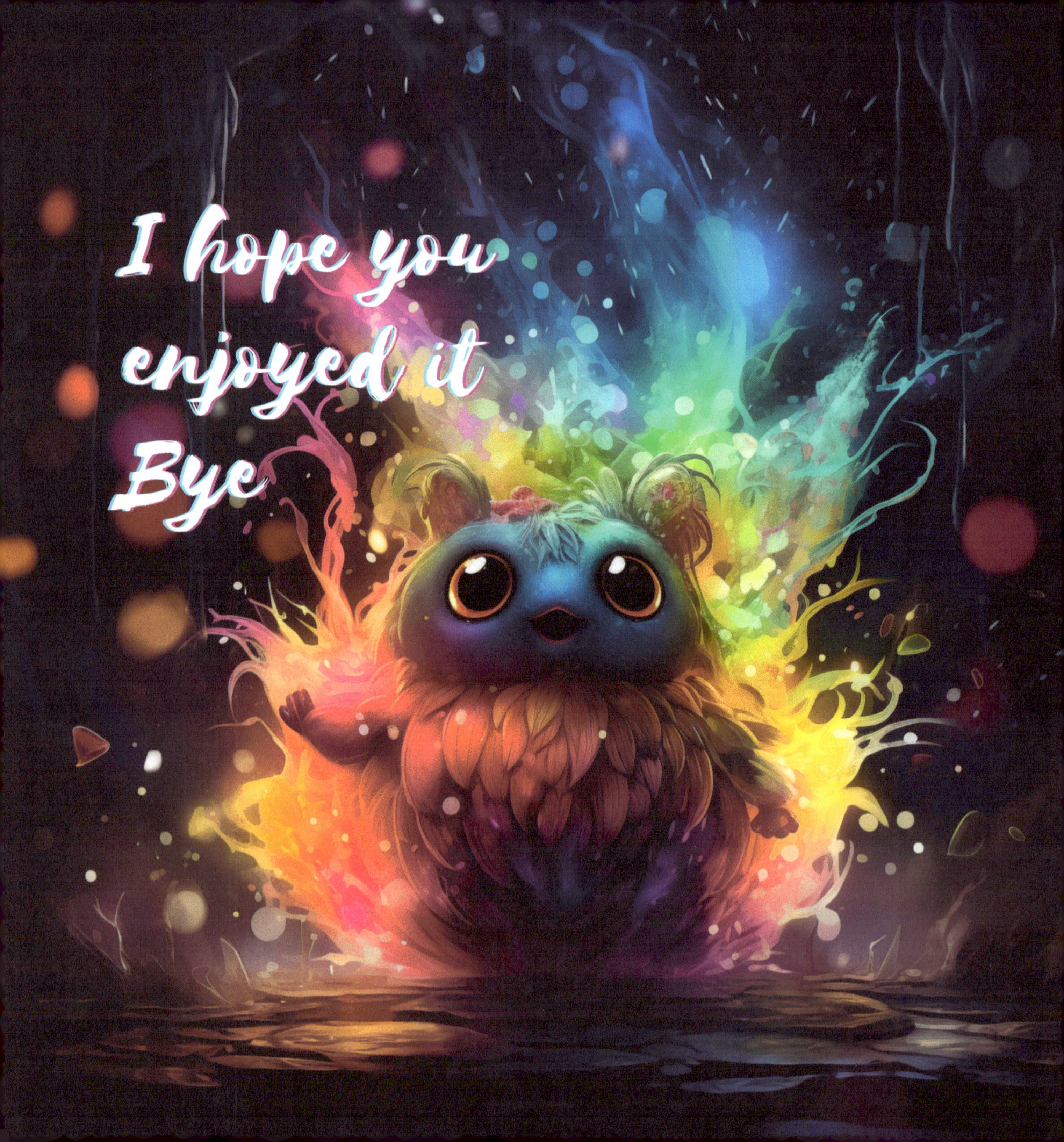
I hope you
enjoyed it
Bye

www.ingramcontent.com/pod-product-compliance
Lightning Source LLC
Chambersburg PA
CBHW041525280526
45792CB00004B/1378
9798868313899